CHARLES T. SMITH

ways to plan & organize your Sunday School

children · grades 1 to 6

INTERNATIONAL CENTER FOR LEARNING

A Division of G/L Publications, Glendale, California, U.S.A.

Photo Credits: Page vii: H. Armstrong Roberts. Page 20, 38, 56, 70, 106: Phil Knepper. Page 88: Doug Gilbert.

Published by Regal Books Division, G/L Publications, Glendale, California 91209, U.S.A.

Library of Congress Catalog Card No. 71-168839. ISBN 0-8307-0123-0

CONTENTS

Preface

Bibliography

Training materials (see catalog) for use with this handbook
are available from your church supplier.

THE AUTHOR

Charles T. Smith holds a BA degree from Western Baptist Bible College and an M.R.E. degree from Talbot Theological Seminary.

He is the Minister of Christian Education at the First Baptist Church of Van Nuys, California, where Sunday school attendance is averaging 3500 weekly. Previously, as Children's Director, he coordinated the work of 250 teachers and officers in the Children's Division of the church. His present ministry also includes speaking and leadership assignments in Sunday schools, seminars and conferences. Charles and Barbara have one daughter.

FOREWORD

The late Dr. Henrietta C. Mears, founder of Gospel Light Publications and distinguished Christian education leader for more than 40 years, often said, "Good teachers are not born; they are made by conscientious labor." It is axiomatic that if one is to be successful in any field, he must be trained. Our Lord recognized this fact in training the Twelve. First He spent the whole night in prayer in preparation for the momentous task of choosing them. From this point the teaching and training of these men became a matter of paramount importance to Him.

A tremendous passion for the training of leadership has been a hallmark in the program of Gospel Light. What workers learn today will determine what the church will be tomorrow. This is the great need of the hour: To train leaders for Christian service, particularly for the Sunday school, who will know how to administer and teach. With a deep sense of obligation as well as opportunity the International Center for Learning was created in 1970 to specialize in the training of dedicated personnel in all departments of the local church.

This is one of a series of textbooks designed to train workers in the Sunday school. It has grown out of actual proven experience and represents the best in educational philosophy. In addition to textual materials, the full program of ICL includes audiovisual media and church leadership training seminars sponsored in strategic centers across America and ultimately overseas as rapidly as God enables. We are being deluged with requests to help in the momentous task of training workers. We dare not stop short of providing all possible assistance.

Train for Sunday school success! Train for church growth! Train people by example and experience to pray and plan and perform. Christ trained the Twelve. Dare we do less?

President
Gospel Light Publications

Who is responsible for the education of our children? Historically, three separate institutions have contested for this right and duty—the state, church and home. Norman DeJong, in his book, *Education in the Truth,* has carefully documented this triple emphasis from the time of Moses to the present.

Jehovah told Moses to instruct the Israelites to teach their children His words; education was home and family centered (Deuteronomy 4:9,10). The word *teach* however, meant more than just religious instruction; it encompassed the total educational needs of a person.

In ancient Greece the Spartan government established and controlled formal education, producing a public or state system.

During the Middle Ages Roman Catholicism assumed this task and developed parochial schools throughout Europe.

Finally, in the United States we have had all three forms of education plus a church-supervised Sunday school program, each given legal protection. Regardless of which institution has assumed the educational role, each has schools to meet its objectives.[1]

The biblical viewpoint places upon parents the responsibility of the education and religious training of their children. DeJong points out that in the comparatively uncomplicated life of the Israelites, most instruction could be accomplished through the home. In New Testament times life had grown more complex, and the greater demands of society required the delegation of some of the parents' educational functions. Yet Paul was insistent that parents were still responsible for bringing their children up "in the nurture and admonition of the Lord" (Ephesians 6:4).

Furthermore, Paul charged church leadership with their duty in religious education—a direct result of the Great Commission (Matthew 28:19, 20).

Apparently the parents in the New Testament church would, in the Old Testament pattern, teach their children. Children of believers were to be a definite concern of the church, for on numerous occasions Paul spoke of the importance of their family role and behavior. In order for a man to qualify for leadership in the church his children had to be well behaved and obedient

(1 Timothy 3:4, 5, 12). Twice Paul directs children to obey their parents in everything, since such behavior pleases God.

The church's educational ministry would not displace parental responsibility but serve to complement and expand it.

For the church to express concern only for believers' children, however, would be to neglect the largest body of children. The Bible stresses reaching children through their parents. Unfortunately, the twentieth century church has frequently put its emphasis in the other direction. It is true that children are more easily reached by the church, but unless parents are also won the child's Christian education is likely to be severely handicapped.

However, many parents have been found to be rocky soil for spiritual seed. Such indifference needs to be countered by the church. Children of spiritually negligent parents may be enrolled in a Bible class, exposed to Christian personalities and the Scriptures. In this way these children may be spiritually nurtured, eventually to the point of salvation and genuine Christian growth.

It was concern for children lacking Christian parental instruction that motivated an English journalist, Robert Raikes, to begin the Sunday school movement almost two hundred years ago. The Bible was taught to develop character in the neglected street urchins of Gloucester. With a hired teacher, a pupil age span of from six through fourteen, a kitchen for the classroom and a six-and-one-half-hour Sunday session, the school was off to a humble beginning. By the time of Raikes' death in 1811 Sunday schools had been widely established in England with a total attendance of 400,000.

From the outset, there was little or no fear on the part of church leaders that the Sunday school would supplant the parents' role in religious instructions. In fact, once such schools were accepted by churches (beginning around 1814) they were seen as a means of accomplishing what public schools were giving up—religious instruction.[2]

In 1861 the book *The Teacher Taught* appeared and clearly pointed out the role this new church agency would play in the church's educational mission. Those parents who would feel that their duty was done when they sent their children to school were those whose children would probably be without any moral or religious training at all were it not for the Sunday school.[3]

The author went on to encourage parents to instruct their children in religion, adding that the Sunday school could still be a very worthwhile supplement to home instructions because of its specialized facilities.

In summary then, the Sunday school was to assist parents in at least three ways: 1) It would serve to guide parents to fulfill their God-given teaching role; 2) It would provide instruction for children who had parents who were negligent in their teaching responsibilities; 3) It would supplement the parents' role through specialized facilities generally unavailable to parents.

These functions of the Sunday school remain unchanged in the 1970's and continue to have great biblical and spiritual relevance. From birth to 18 years of age a child has approximately 90,000 waking hours. Of these hours, 78,000 are spent within the home, 10,000 in school (not counting extracurricular activities), and only 2,000 in the church (if he attends regularly). To put it in business language, the parents are the major stockholders and have the controlling interest in the education of their children. It would be foolish to assume that Sunday schools could ever totally replace the influence of home teaching or the parents' primary role in religious training.

The Sunday school can and must, however, augment the home, providing professional classroom instruction as well as guidance for parents in improving their role. In this way the Sunday school becomes a partner with the parents in the Christian education of their children—a true biblical function for the church of Jesus Christ.

FOOTNOTES

PREFACE

1 · Norman DeJong, *Education in the Truth* (Nuttey, N.J.: Presbyterian and Reformed Publishing Co., 1969), pp. 120-123.

2 · J. Donald Butler, *Religious Education, the Foundation and Practice of Nurture* (New York: Harper and Row Publishers, 1961), pp. 60-63; and C. B. Eavey, *History of Christian Education* (Chicago: Moody Press, 1964), pp. 223-227.

3 · *The Teacher Taught* (Philadelphia: American Sunday School Union, 1861), p. 195.

A NEW WORLD FOR CHILDREN

Christian parents have a biblical mandate to which they should adhere: "Train up a child in the way he should go: and when he is old, he will not depart from it" (Proverbs 22:6). This training process is accomplished primarily through the home, since the parents have their children first and most. However, groups of Christian parents may effectively augment home training by organizing Bible classes geared to meet age level needs and to provide the stimulus that comes through group learning processes.

John Chrysostom, who served as the bishop of Antioch during the first century, emphasized the importance of this biblical mandate: "If good precepts are impressed on the soul while it is yet tender, no man will be able to destroy them when they have set firm, even as does a waxen seal. Make use of his life as thou shouldest. Thou wilt be the first to benefit, if thou hast a good son, and then God."[1]

Chrysostom went on to describe the methods to use in such training. He felt that children should be sheltered from certain evil influences and be under constant guidance. He noted the importance of a good learning environment and encouraged the use of almost all of a child's senses in this training process.

Moreover, this spiritual leader was concerned over the child neglect he saw in his own culture. At this point of cultural need both the first century and the twentieth century seem to meet. "In our own day," writes Chrysostom, "every man takes the greatest pains to train his boy in the arts and in literature and speech [liberal arts, athletics and art of TV viewing]. But to exercise this child's soul in virtue, to that no man any longer pays heed."[3]

MONTAGE OF THE MODERN CHILD

In some respects children are the same from one generation to the next.

There are some things, however, which distinguish the children of this decade from previous ones. We tend to view childhood in terms of our own childhood or our own immediate Christian family situation. Our society has changed in many ways in just one generation, producing conditions of which many adults may not yet be aware. The combination of the following pictures of the modern world of childhood provides for us a montage that should strengthen our understanding of them and enhance our teaching ministry to them.

FAMILY SURVIVAL?

Today's children are products of the present life-style of our society, of the feelings, attitudes and tastes of our nation. Several things characterize this culture.

First, it is one in which the basic unit of society, the family, is struggling for survival. *Time* magazine's article "The American Family: Future Uncertain,"[4] carefully documents the present family crisis; a portion of these findings resulted from the December 1970 White House Conference on Children.

The support for the claims of family failure is mammoth. One in every four marriages eventually ends in divorce. The divorce rate is rising even higher among more recent marriages.

The major factor contributing to the present family crisis is said to be the woman's changing role. Formerly, wives as mothers and keepers of the home supplemented the husband's role. Now that forty percent of the American women are employed, they tend to have a new perception of themselves. Their expectations and frustrations are greater. Certain home obligations (including child care) have, of necessity, been farmed out to others.

Often the mother works because of the desire to provide more fully for what she considers to be family needs. Without realizing it, however, she may actually be neglecting her children, the very objects of her "sacrifice."

Each couple must carefully weigh their circumstances before committing themselves to extra employment or other extracurricular projects that may prove detrimental to their children's well-being.

In some families where two incomes are a necessity, the mother has found work during the hours when her children were in school or when her husband could be home with the children. The most important thing in these situations is that parents do all they can to keep disruption of their normal family life at a minimum.

ELECTRONIC COMMUNICATION

Our culture is one of electronic communication—transistor radio, television, phonograph records, tapes, movies, and even pictures in newspapers. World happenings are rapidly communicated to our children so that they live in the middle of history-making events. Previously the child's world included only community or national events. Now the whole world is before him!

Such communication changes our children. They view their world differently. Their aspirations for life are affected. Attitudes toward human need, parents, violence and love are all molded through the mass media. This is especially true when you realize that it is estimated that a "child watches 17,000 hours of TV before the age of eighteen—more than 60 percent of time spent in the classroom."[5]

Electronic communication is also, however, a menace of staggering proportions. It is true that it has its distinct advantages of educating children, but it has also served to stimulate them in ways which are totally undesirable. The increased hate, violence, materialism, sexual permissiveness and general rise in un-Christ-like attitudes and behavior have been partly fostered by the mass media.

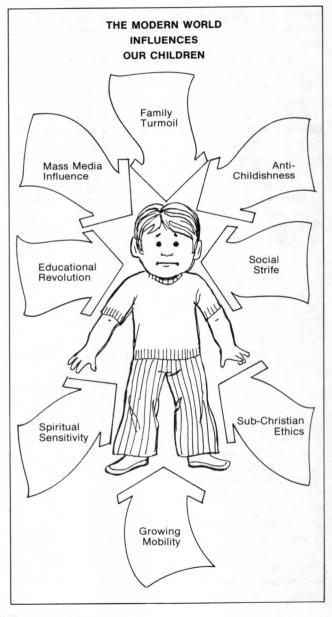

**THE MODERN WORLD
INFLUENCES
OUR CHILDREN**

Family
Turmoil

Mass Media
Influence

Anti-
Childishness

Educational
Revolution

Social
Strife

Spiritual
Sensitivity

Sub-Christian
Ethics

Growing
Mobility

Official studies have shown the killings on television average almost one per hour, and the incidents of violence one every 22 minutes. One survey revealed that 10 A.M. to noon on Saturdays—the prime viewing time for children—is the prime time for violence also. These two hours of viewing were generally cartoons that possessed high aggressive content, filled with killings, beatings, monsters, poor science fiction and fantasy.[6]

GROWING MOBILITY

The present culture is one of great mobility. In a typical year during the 1960s more than 35 million Americans moved. Over 22 million moved within the same county. Slightly over 6 million others moved within the same state.[7]

In other words, 41 percent—nearly one-half of the entire nation between 20 and 24 years of age—moved in one year. Three of ten family units between 25 and 34 moved within the same year.

Mobility in the seventies is expected to be even greater. More people will be moving more often with less chance for them to establish roots in a community before moving again.

What are the results upon our children of such mobility? Stability of family life is affected. Close human and community relationships have little time to develop under such circumstances. Children, having just established themselves with their peers in school, church and neighborhood, and with their doctors and dentists, must suddenly be transplanted to a totally new area. Insecurity may develop with a child who does not make friends easily.[8]

Unfortunately, families are simultaneously getting away from the influence of the traditional church ministry or program. Thus, attendance at church and Sunday school is interrupted and so is the formal process of Christian education. Loyalty to Christian convictions and vitality in Christian experience may subtly be undermined. Under these circumstances the Sunday school teacher's job becomes all the more difficult and challenging.

POST-CHRISTIAN ETHICS

Our children are living in a culture that is post-Christian. Ethically, our culture does not support the traditional Christian code of morality held by our nation from the time of its founding. The rapid trend toward moral decay and corruption in all realms of society is something that has been accepted as a matter of fact.

Our children are being raised in a society that glamorizes premarital and extramarital sex, condones homosexuality and abortion, makes divorce easy, stimulates drug abuse and permits trashy magazines and films to exist.

It is true that many non-Christian people do hold to certain Christian standards of conduct. In a lecture to a 1970 Youth Conference in Pennsylvania, Dr. Francis A. Schaeffer referred to them as the "silent majority," since they hold to the Christian ethic but not to that ethic's foundational source, the Bible. Thus, their children are taught the ethic but not the source of its authority. As a result the ethic is often rejected in adolescence as something merely traditional that may be dispensed with without repercussion.

Furthermore, this moral climate is one in which there are no absolutes—no real "rights" or "wrongs." Everything, seemingly, is relative (dependent on the situation, not on moral law). This moral confusion and anarchy produces a hopeless, degenerate post-Christian attitude and behavior. This is especially true when there exists an empty or sickly spiritual nature on the part of parents, making them incapable of defensive or offensive action.

SOCIAL TURMOIL

Another part of our montage of modern childhood is our present social turmoil, both national and international. Integration, desegregation, school bussing, civil rights and wrongs and minority grievances are situations constantly put before our children. They are aware of the inequalities that exist, especially when they reach middle and older childhood (third through sixth grade).

Children have naturally adopted adult attitudes and convictions on racial matters. Unfortunately, many professing Christians have responded to this national crisis in racial ways, not scripturally. On such a fundamental issue believers, parents and Sunday school teachers need to stand firmly upon their only source of authority for faith and life—the Word of God—and not upon their upbringing or emotions. By doing so they will provide a healthy model that will be imitated by the observing child.

Our social climate is also one of individual and national conflict. Christ warned us of that end time which would be marked by "wars and rumors of wars." We certainly have this situation today. The everyday details of such turmoil are readily available to our children via television. The stench of hate, killing and death reaches our children and may either desensitize them toward such destruction or provide a foundation for instruction in a healthier Christian world view or perspective. A portion of such instruction should be provided through the Sunday school.

The social turmoil is also evident between generations. The idea of a generation gap may be something that has been overdone, but the "now generation"—the generation that our children will soon be joining and modifying—does feel estranged from adults who think and act in traditional ways. This new generation has sought to distinguish itself from the older one, both in appearance and life-style.

Already we are aware of the increased social sophistication of the preadolescent (older junior), something extracted from information gained through the mass media. Our present culture is forcing upon our children more "youthfulness" in attitudes and behavior. They are dressing older, dating earlier and maturing emotionally to the point that some are manifesting certain adult emotional disorders. The Christian social-moral challenge is before us!

ANTICHILDISHNESS

According to many educators and psychologists, fewer and fewer children are enjoying childhood. In her book *The Conspiracy Against Childhood,* Eda J. LeShan graphically tells how children are being robbed of their birthright. They walk a tightrope between neglect and pressure. Either they get too much stimulation or none at all. The rate of child suicides mounts each year, and there are increasing accounts of diseases associated with tension—ulcers, colitis, migraine, falling hair and asthma.

Part of this present child climate is due to the urge of parents to see their children "grow up." They are thinking primarily of what their children will someday become—adults—rather than what they are now—children. The noisiness and messiness of childhood are disliked, so the children are liked best when they act like adults. The adult teacher wants the children to sit down and be quiet, to produce, to conform, to be mini-adults.

Adultlike pressures are brought upon the children; they must be put through the paces just like their parents. They should excel in everything, matching the achievements of other children, adjusting as well socially as their peers and having a high I.Q.

Thus an enormous new burden is placed upon children. We want them to love us all the time, to be respectful, well adjusted and interesting; to be happy, to learn quickly, be studious and athletic.

To sum it up, Mrs. LeShan feels that we are trying to eliminate childhood. Every stage of childhood is, however, vital to ultimate psychological, physical, intellectual and social well-being. "An anti-child social climate," she writes, "robs our children of what is most natural and human in themselves, and dooms us all to a terrible impoverishment of the spirit."[9]

It is crucial that those teaching in a children's Sunday school department realize that their pupils should be expected to think, act and respond like children—not adults.

There are, on the other hand, thousands of children who are not pressured to excel, but are greatly neglected. They are left to fend for themselves in a difficult world, a hard task even for those best prepared for it. Howard James, in his shocking book, *Children in Trouble: A National Scandal,* tells how unbelievably primitive and brutal institutions have been to children who were neglected, delinquent, retarded or emotionally disturbed. He spent a year covering America gathering this information. The startling facts of his investigation caused him to be subjected to smear tactics, threats and personal abuse, all to cover up his horrible findings.[10]

Affluence is certainly no cure-all. Parental neglect visits children in every strata of our society, even in Christian homes. You have heard of "good" parents who have been so wrapped up in their little world—be it business, social or church—that they had little of themselves left to make available to their children.

EDUCATIONAL REVOLUTION

This decade is also one of dramatic changes in the child's public education. New methods of teaching, more flexible classroom organization, and greater responsiveness to parental and social concerns are general areas of thrust in this basic institution.

New approaches toward the teaching of the traditional three "R's" have, among other things, resulted in the "new math," the "code-emphasis approach" of teaching reading (improved phonics method), and the "new English" and new methods of teaching foreign languages.

A less formal and rigid approach toward pupil and curriculum has also evolved. More imaginative and flexible approaches of presenting subject matter have resulted in improved learning.

Educational leaders have called for movement away from a rote, routine and authoritarian classroom atmosphere. In its place a genuine discovery method and child-generated interest in learning are encouraged.

Technology has brought about teaching machines for programmed curriculum material. Associated with this development is the programmed textbook which is also used in some children's Christian education curriculum. Individualized instruction is enhanced through such programmed material, allowing for a pupil to progress at his own rate of speed, interest and capability.

Independent study, team teaching and ability groupings are also employed to facilitate the learning process. It is estimated that independent study will play an even greater role in years to come, consuming a good portion of each school day.

Learning centers (language arts, science, reading, geography) are aiding in making such independent study, as well as small group study, effective. Various types of materials and equipment are used, including cassette or tape recorders, earphones for private or small group listening, and filmstrip, microscope and filmloop (cassette) projectors, phonographs, books and art supplies. These centers serve as alternatives to the traditional concept of seat work in which children sat at their desks all or most of the time using dittoed work sheets or workbooks. The children assume more responsibility for self-direction and are allowed some choice as to their activities each day.

Team teaching is being utilized in many elementary schools to improve the teaching of specific subjects and to put to greater use the areas of individual teacher skill. The inherent weakness of this plan is that children are frequently unable to relate well to three or four different teachers each day.

Educators, hoping to change the traditional classroom environment, are recommending schools without walls and accompanying programs that will promote the utilization of the total community-environmental resources (newspaper and telephone offices, bakeries, dairies, radio and television stations, airports, botanical gardens, city cultural centers and museums) to offset a regimented educational organization. The goal is to make school life as exciting as the outside world by freeing children from architecturally confining and monotonous classrooms.

As this type of public school environment becomes more common, one wonders if our children might have the tendency to turn off our message in the traditional Sunday school environment, which would seem dull and restrictive by comparison.

Secular educators are aware that if healthy, vibrant personal relationships are not developed between teacher and pupils and if the curriculum is not geared to individual needs, modern teaching technology, methods and environment will fail to meet expectations.

A concerned Sunday school teacher who develops a meaningful relationship with his pupils and simultaneously guides pupils in the study of relevant Bible content will do much to offset shortcomings in technology and general educational environment.

SPIRITUAL AWARENESS

Our children are living in a society replete with religious forms and activity. More than 60 percent of the people who live in single-family dwellings are affiliated with a local church or synagogue.

Furthermore, there is a growing noninstitutional religious movement outside of the church and considerable interest in Eastern religions and mystical philosophy as well as spiritism and astrology. All of these visible activities are manifestations of a spiritual awareness.

Our children hear and see these expressions of the religious nature of men and women. If they do not imitate them, they are certainly conditioned towards the God-idea and the realization of something or someone beyond the material world in which they live. Being raised in an atheistic home might nullify this realization for some children. Nevertheless, the great majority of children will demonstrate a spiritual awareness that is prompted by our religious culture.

A younger child's thinking process makes it difficult for him to comprehend some of the abstractions in the Bible. For example, most children identify the term *church* with a specific congregation or building. They also are unable to distinguish between Jesus, God and the Holy Spirit. Furthermore, they struggle in understanding baptism and the Lord's Supper.

Older juniors are moving into the stage of abstract thinking. They are beginning to reason abstractly and are able to grasp certain doctrinal or theological truths that were previously intellectually unattainable. At this point our children are particularly open to a more meaningful conversion experience, especially if they are from a Christian home.

Over 25 percent of the teenagers surveyed by the National Sunday School Association in 1968 indicated that they received Christ as Saviour between nine and eleven years of age.[11] Since every child develops at a different rate, it should not be assumed, however, that decisions for Christ prior to this age are premature, nor that indecision at this age is abnormal. Sunday school teachers will want to be particularly sensitive to each child's intellectual-spiritual readiness regarding this important step.

MEANINGFUL OBJECTIVES IN TEACHING THE MODERN CHILD

Although the world which surrounds our children is rapidly undergoing change, the basic purposes of churches seeking to minister to them remain the same. According to the last seven verses of Acts, chapter two, there are five distinct functions that the church had in its original form: 1) To educate; 2) To fellowship; 3) To worship; 4) To serve or minister; 5) To evangelize. All of these functions brought glory to God—the ultimate purpose of the Christian individually and corporately.

You who teach children should express a broad concern for your pupils—one which encompasses these stated functions of the church as well as the needs of the whole child. To merely "save a child's soul" comes short of the all-inclusive aim of Christian education, "that the man of God may be perfect, thoroughly furnished unto all good works" (2 Timothy 3:17). It is obvious that this objective is an ultimate one, but one which we should keep in mind as we teach our children. The end of all such instruction is Christian maturation and practical holiness.

BIBLICAL OBJECTIVES IN TEACHING CHILDREN

1. Foundational Bible Instruction
2. Instruction Towards Salvation
3. Instruction in Worship
4. Instruction in Ministry
5. Instruction in Sharing Christ

FOUNDATIONAL BIBLE INSTRUCTION

We have already seen that instruction in God's Word was to begin in the early years of childhood (Deuteronomy 4:9,10). The family was the first school and the parents the first teachers. Josephus wrote that, "Above all we pride ourselves on the education of our children, and regard as the most essential task in life the observance of our laws and of the pious practices, based thereupon, which we inherited."[12]

Children were taught from "swaddling clothes" to recognize "God as Father and Maker of the world" even before the normal instruction in the Law by parents and teachers.[13]

It is of vital importance that teachers realize that one of their key objectives in teaching children is to lay a foundation upon which the children may live now as well as in the future. Children must grow in their understanding of who God is, what He has done and how He wants them to live. This may be accomplished by the wise communication of God's Word in the time that is ours in Sunday school and through other opportunities in the church life.

INSTRUCTION TOWARDS SALVATION

As we continue to teach our children they will individually come to the point in time when they truly perceive themselves as separated from God because of their sin. They will see Jesus Christ as God's own Son, Who loved them so much that He died for all the bad things they ever did and will do. Furthermore, they will know that believing in Christ as their Saviour from the penalty of sin is the only way they can become a member of God's family (John 1:12) and someday go to heaven (John 14:1-6). Such truths need to be repeatedly taught to these pupils, following these five principles:

1   Every child should be dealt with individually. This will avoid the problem of a child responding because others in the class are desiring to make this decision.

2   Each child's religious background should be taken into consideration. Does he come from a Christian home? If so, he may be better prepared to make this decision due to the increased amount of spiritual ex-

posure, both through the home and the church.

3   Each child must have the gospel explained in terms understandable to him. Are the scriptural expressions you use to explain the good news those he is familiar with and understands (sin, salvation, eternal life, believe)? Avoid the use of symbolic terms (washed in His blood, let Jesus come into your heart) to facilitate his understanding.

Marjorie Soderholm suggests following this five point guide: a) "God loves you." b) "You have sinned." c) "Christ died to pay for your sin." d) "You must admit to Him that you are a sinner and ask Him to forgive you." e) "Then you are in God's family and you have everlasting life."[14]

4   Each child should be asked questions to be certain he understands salvation. These questions should require more than a yes or no answer, since even the most undiscriminating child may be able to shake his head in the right direction. To discern if the child understands what a "sinner" is, for example, he might be asked the difference between disobeying God and disobeying adult authority. A child needs to see "sin" as something that is bigger than not following the prohibitions of his parents. Disobedience to parents is an evidence of a greater sin problem. To break away from the parental-labeled sins you might ask a pupil, "What have you done wrong that has hurt God and made Him unhappy?" Now sin is identified as something that displeases God and not merely the pupil's parents.

Not only does a child need to have a proper sense of sin, but through careful questioning we should seek to discover if he understands the following concepts: a) How Jesus saves a person; b) What it means to be forgiven; c) The personal acceptance of Christ's death for him; and d) The commitment of himself to Jesus—following Him in discipleship.[15]

We are aware that each child will come to the realization of his need to receive Christ at a different time. Forcing a decision upon a child may be likened to the attempt to force a butterfly out of its cocoon too soon; it can be crippled. Prayerful patience and spiritual alertness on the part of children's teachers will aid in sensing each child's readiness for this all-important decision.

5   Each child's decision should be preceded by the use of the Bible in counselling and crystallized through a personal prayer. The child needs to see the Bible as the source of our knowledge about salvation and how it takes place. He should be directed to only a few verses of relevant Scripture (John 1:12; John 3:16; Romans 3:23; 5:8) so that any confusion might be eliminated. A modern language New Testament will aid a child in understanding such verses, though a simple explanation or amplification of the same references in the King James Version will be adequate.

AFTER CONVERSION—WHAT

A child is likely to express apprehension about praying to receive Christ as his Saviour. You may need to suggest certain expressions his prayer might include: 1) Acknowledgment of his sinfulness—"God, I know that I have done bad things and haven't pleased You." 2) Recognition of the redemptive work of Christ on his behalf—"I thank You that You sent your Son to take my punishment for all the bad things I have done." 3) Acceptance of Christ as his only Saviour—"Right now I want to become a member of your family by accepting Jesus as my Saviour."

Be careful to let each child express himself in his own way; we want his prayer of faith to be meaningful to him, even though it may lack some of the certainty of an adult. God knows the child's heart.

The child's prayer may be followed by a brief time of questions and answers with related conversation to further clarify his decision. "What happened to you when you accepted Jesus as your Saviour?" "Did God forgive you of your sin?" "What kind of life did God just give you?" A prayer of thanksgiving may be offered by the teacher as a fitting conclusion to this significant experience. Do not forget to encourage this child in his new family relationship; he needs our prayers and spiritual nurturing.

INSTRUCTION IN WORSHIP

Our children from the beginning of our instruction need

to become aware of God's reality and presence. They need to sense His worth and express it in ways meaningful to them. It may be through a prayer, a song, a minute of silence, or through drawing or painting a picture of something God has made or done.

The church will be seen as the place where Christians come together to worship God at least once a week. The pastor's sermon, the congregational hymns and .choir should be seen as ways which assist people in worshipping. Younger children will have difficulty in comprehending the meaning of such worship activities as baptism and the Lord's Supper due to the child's concrete, literal thinking level. These ordinances may be understood only as rites commanded by Jesus and therefore necessary for His followers to practice.

Yet worship should be understood as a personal attitude toward God and His creation that one possesses whenever he is away from the church building as well. Children should grow to understand the many ways they may express this worship of God outside of the Sunday school department. Their lives should be constant expressions of such worship: obeying God's commandments, praying, appreciating nature as God's creation, reading and memorizing God's Word and telling others about Christ. Establishing the habit of daily Bible reading and talking to God is something each teacher of junior children should set as worship goals for his pupils.

INSTRUCTION IN MINISTRY

When the early church members shared their possessions with one another, they were expressing a deep sense of worth and thankfulness toward God's goodness in salvation. When, as God's people, they responded to the needs around them, they became true "ministers"—servants of Christ. Christ had set the right example for such a ministry when He washed the disciples' feet.

Our children are certainly capable of such acts of ministry. Think of the many needy and confined people who could be refreshed by simple acts of childhood kindness and affection. Many children's Sunday school classes have been used to bring such encouragement.

The wise teacher will lead his children to discover ways to adequately minister both corporately and individually. No doubt the greatest opportunities a child has to help, encourage and share with others are found within the day-to-day experiences among his peers—the most difficult place in which to serve. Our teaching content will take on special significance educationally when our pupils are led to behave like Christians in such a real-life context.

INSTRUCTION IN SHARING CHRIST

Simply stated, the purpose of the church includes: education and missions. The first takes place within the church, and the latter outside the church, although there is of necessity some crossing over in the context of these purposes. Furthermore, good Christian education cannot take place without involvement in missions, nor missions without education. From the outset our children need to see missions—sharing Christ—as a natural part of the Christian life. Even though they may not have yet received Christ as Saviour, children can share Christ with others in simple ways. Through home and church instruction a child's outlook on life, attitudes and behavior are shaped and nurtured in the Christian direction even without his personal commitment to this way of life; this is as it should be. A child's prayer at mealtime may be a subtle testimony to unsaved guests. His exuberant singing of "Jesus Loves Me" or "I Love to Go to Church" may carry a similar message to childhood friends.

In the truest sense, however, sharing Christ is something accomplished by the Christian child in his relationships and contacts with the unsaved. As our children meet Christ in the experience of conversion, they will be alive to the fact that their friends must also know Jesus. Teachers must guide these children in exploring the avenues through which they may lead their friends to Christ. For many children their first overt act as a "missionary" is through bringing an acquaintance to a home Bible class or to Sunday school. More individual direct sharing between the Christian child and the non-Christian child should be encouraged.

Evangelism will also encompass not only the immediate world of the child but the whole world as well. Christ's Great Commission must be taught and its contemporary outworkings and effects carefully described. Missions is an exciting subject for our children, especially our juniors with their growing worldwide consciousness. People everywhere must hear about Jesus and accept Him as their Saviour too. Seeing, hearing and personally meeting missionaries will greatly aid our children in comprehending the importance of the missionary task.

All of the above objectives in teaching children in the Sunday school are based on and rooted in the Bible. Nothing is as important as communicating the truths of this living Book to our children and then leading them to function as part of the church community. Since our children are *children* and not adolescents or adults, we must carefully guide them in their own exploration and rate of comprehension of all that God expects from Christians. This writer trusts that you have been awed by this task and yet drawn and attracted to the importance of meeting the challenge of teaching God's truth to today's children.

FOOTNOTES

CHAPTER 1

1 · Kendig Brubaker Cully, ed., *Basic Writings in Christian Education* (Philadelphia: The Westminster Press, 1960), pp. 52-53.

2 · Cully, *Basic Writings in Christian Education,* pp. 55-59.

3 · Cully, *Basic Writings in Christian Education,* p. 52.

4 · Leon Jaroff, ed., Ingrid Michaelis, and others, "The American Family: Future Uncertain," *Time,* December 28, 1970, pp. 34-35.

5 · D. Keith Osborn and William Hale, "Television Violence," *Childhood Education,* vol. 45, no. 9, May 1969, p. 507.

6 · Osborn and Hale, "Television Violence," p. 506.

7 · Wayne M. Warner, "Making Moving More Meaningful," *Home Life,* August 1970, p. 29.

8 · B. A. Clendinning, Jr., ed., *Family Ministry in Today's Church* (Nashville: Convention Press, 1971), pp. 12-13.

9 · Eda J. LeShan, *The Conspiracy Against Childhood* (New York: Atheneum, 1967), pp. 5-9, 12, 36, 39.

10 · Howard James, *Children in Trouble: A National Scandal* (New York: David McKay Co., 1970).

11 · Roy B. Zuck and Gene A. Getz, *Christian Youth, an In-Depth Study* (Chicago: Moody Press, 1968), pp. 40-41.

12 · Robert Ulich, *A History of Religious Education* (New York: University Press, 1968), p. 8.

13 · C. B. Eavy, *History of Christian Education* (Chicago: Moody Press, 1964), p. 52.

14 · Marjorie Soderholm, *Explaining Salvation to Children* (Minneapolis: Free Church Publications, 1962), pp. 10-11.

15 · LaVerne Ashby, "Primaries and Church Membership," *Baptist Training Union Magazine,* March 1970, pp. 56-59.

BIBLE TEACHING TODAY

Breaking into the latter part of the twentieth century is Christ's first century command: "Go therefore and make disciples of all the nations . . . teaching them to observe all that I commanded you . . ." (see Matthew 28:19,20). The teaching our Saviour demands is packed with results. He saw the necessity of pupils experiencing the truths being communicated. They were to be taught to keep and practice all of Christ's commandments. Teaching of this quality is hard to come by but obviously it is vital and strategic to the fulfillment of the Saviour's deepest intentions and plan.

Such teaching is not likely to result from simply telling a Bible story to our children. Certainly this is possible, since God's Word is dynamic. But under today's normal teaching circumstances, a Sunday school teacher must do more than repeat the story in the quarterly to move his pupils to live the truth involved.

UNIQUE TEACHING METHODS

The Old Testament prophets were our contemporaries in this respect; they had extreme difficulty in getting through to the lives of those they sought to teach. Generally, mere verbal communication—"telling the story"—did not result in changed attitudes or behavior. They employed more dramatic methods to gain the attention of their hearers. Sometimes they played the role of a wandering minstrel, singing popular songs. Or, like

Isaiah, they walked the streets naked and in chains to warn the sinning people of impending bondage by a foreign power. Micah went from village to village crying the names of the towns and using puns upon their names, like "weep now in Weep-Town" and "dust now in Dust-Town."

Despite such efforts these prophets found that the people generally did not choose to live according to God's commandments.

Is there a lesson to be learned in this by Sunday school teachers? Yes. Teaching that causes individuals to practice God's commandments is not easily accomplished; it is the most difficult part of the teaching/learning process.

Centuries later, a new "prophet" also encountered such difficulties in teaching. Although Jesus taught with authority, His methods in instruction allowed for individual freedom in exploring and discovering the truths He desired to teach. He thoroughly understood the inner workings of the human heart and mind and how to deal with them.

He employed a variety of teaching methods. His informal conversations with small groups included questions and answers, dialogue, discussion and storytelling. He used proverbs—simple, vivid statements about difficult subjects ("The first shall be last and the last first," for example) and parables—stories with simple surface meanings that also suggested truths of deeper spiritual significance (like the parable of the Good Samaritan).

Demonstrations—observable experiences or events— were used to show the disciples His character (Matthew 11:2-19). Activities were used in order to provide the firsthand experiences so essential to more permanent learning. Jesus sent out His disciples, both the twelve (Matthew 10:1-42, Luke 9:1-6) and the seventy (Luke 10:1-12,17) to put into practice much of what He had been teaching them. He was aware of the value of such activity. They would encounter all types of situations that would result in their own spiritual growth.

Furthermore, Jesus followed specific principles in His practice of teaching. First, He normally started on a personal level (John 4:7). Second, His teaching content was related to the needs of those He taught (Matthew 5:3-11). Third, His teaching approach and pattern did not become stereotyped. Fourth, He used the principle of apperception: He began with, and built upon, an individual's present knowledge and experience. Fifth, He secured the person's self-activity by encouraging questions, asking questions and creating a problem-solving spirit. Sixth, He encouraged learning by doing, thus achieving a remarkable continuity between head knowledge (content) and experiential knowledge (practice) within his pupils.[1]

OLD AND NEW VIEWS OF TEACHING AND LEARNING

Most Sunday school teachers do not entirely adopt the teaching/learning process the way Christ practiced it. His freedom in employing all types of methods, His personalized approach, His pupil-related content, His ability to excite pupil self-activity and action all seem to act as a mirror for our own teaching skill. Our reflected shortcomings leave us standing in awe of the Master. For those of us who have taught for some time and have attended countless Sunday school conventions and workshops, Christ as a model teacher is a constant challenge.

Let us briefly draw four areas of contrast in the contemporary church educational scene. These contrasts between the old and new in Christian education relate to the roles of the teacher, the pupil, the content and the method.

TEACHER: TELLER VERSUS GUIDE

For a long time those who were teachers in Sunday school viewed their role as one that called for preparing a good lesson and teaching it in such a way as to captivate and maintain the interests of their pupils. In this procedure the pupil was primarily passive—sitting, listening and watching the teacher and from time to time asking or answering questions. The teacher was by far the most active, since he studied, prepared, presented and applied the lesson. He seemed to be the one learning most, since he was doing most of the work—going through the tasks or activities by which we learn best. He was at the center of the learning process while the pupils were at the perimeter.

Note the way Christ taught the woman at the well (John 4). First, He met this woman on her own ground and during her own daily schedule. He initiated their conversation and drew her into a central role, where she was motivated to express her deep racial-religious feelings. Then Jesus promised her "living water"—something that really excited her curiosity. She asked a question regarding this water's source. Through careful guidance, Jesus then pointed her to Himself as the source of the "living water" which quenches the deepest thirst and results in everlasting life. Totally motivated, the woman requested this water! Then Jesus transferred His pupil's thinking from her temporal need to her ultimate spiritual need by asking her to call her husband. In a moment she perceived Jesus to be a prophet and with deep respect was drawn to confess and believe. Furthermore, she immediately went to her friends and shared her testimony, leading them to the Messiah. (Her sharing was done without a single direct exhortation on witnessing!) The teacher wisely guided the student in her personal exploration and discovery of God's truth. Jesus didn't give the Samaritan woman a predigested lesson but guided her to grapple with the truth as it related to her own life. This kind of teaching produces results!

Jesus didn't always play the traditional role of teacher, standing up front and lecturing to His pupils. As the teacher, He drew the pupil into a central role in the exciting adventure of learning. As Cornelius Jaarsma said, "Learning is essentially an activity of the learner."[2]

Furthermore, Christian education should not be viewed as a rigid plan of authoritative indoctrination but as a life-flowing process of what one writer calls, "inoculation." Pupils being taught the Scriptures must at the same time be given small doses of the opposing viewpoint and helped to wrestle with and counteract them in light of Christianity. Generally such new points will be brought into the class by the pupils themselves.

TEACHER AS TELLER

Area of most learning activity

X Teacher inside—active

Pupils on perimeter—passive

TEACHER AS GUIDE

Teacher guiding pupils in effective learning activity

X

Children must be aware of the fact that their beliefs may be subject to attack, and they must be given the opportunity to develop defenses against such attacks.[3] They must, under the guidance of a skilled teacher, learn to struggle firsthand with such real-life problems and discover the spiritual solution. Through practicing such a procedure, our students, like Christ's disciples, will be far better equipped to live successfully.

PUPIL: VESSEL VERSUS PLANT

When the teacher views himself as a teller or dispenser of biblical information, the pupil, as we have pointed out, is generally relegated to the lesser, passive role of listener. He is one who "soaks up the Bible" and at appropriate times has the opportunity to ask questions and discuss matters pertaining to the lesson.

This attitude toward teaching has been called the "mug-jug" theory of education. Basically, this theory pictures the teacher as the "mug" and the pupil as the "jug." Education is then simplified to the process of the "mug" pouring knowledge into the "empty jug." "In this approach," writes Eda J. LeShan, "the child is not helped to relate facts, nor does he learn ways of looking for information, processing, integrating, interpreting or differentiating between facts when he acquires them."[4]

Research in public education has shown that from fifty to seventy-five percent of a child's time in the classroom is spent listening. This fact shows that teachers talk too much and children talk too little.[5] The percentage of time a child spends listening in the Sunday school runs just as high.

It is important, however, that children express themselves through words and other means (creative writing and art, for example), for it enables the teacher to evaluate how and what the children are learning through the various teaching/learning activities. In this approach the pupil is certainly not a vessel to be filled but a freely growing plant that is being nurtured through verbal and nonverbal sharing. You will notice that when Jesus taught the woman at the well, He made only seven statements, while she made six (two in the form of questions); she had an equal share in the verbal activity.

The Pupil . . .

A "jug" to be filled?   or   A "plant" to be nurtured?

Another factor related to the "vessel" pupil role in Sunday school education is physical in nature. Generally, the pupil sits most of the Sunday school hour—something which is contrary to a child's stage of development. "When we demand that the elementary child sit still," states Dr. Ernest Ligon, "he is using all of his energy to control himself and there is no energy left for learning."[6]

Just as various types of plants have differing characteristics in appearance, growth, general care and feeding, so our pupils differ from one another. Some learn best when a discovery (inductive approach) is used, while others will benefit more through a deductive pattern (moving from a particular truth or principle to its various parts and ramifications). Some children learn best when they experience firsthand the truths being taught, while others can accomplish the same end vicariously when it is explained by the teacher. Moreover, some children learn more when their efforts are spaced evenly for short periods of time over an extended session, while others can experience the material in a concentrated period of time once it is impressed upon them.[7]

CONTENT-CENTERED/LIFE-CENTERED

Historically, Sunday schools have majored heavily on Bible content; after all, teaching the Bible is the purpose of these institutions. Within the last decade there has been a great effort made toward balancing biblical "content-centeredness" and pupil "life-centeredness." This balancing effort may have, at times, lacked equilibrium, with a tendency to concentrate more on the data or content of the Bible rather than the application of it to the day-to-day needs of the children.

KEEPING A BALANCE?

The tendency towards a content-centeredness in teaching is also influenced by the "mug-jug" theory of education. Emphasis is upon the biblical data and getting it into the pupil, since the teacher knows it has life-transforming potential. The truth Jesus taught was always appropriate for the occasion and the pupils involved. In fact, He once terminated the communication of some theological information to His disciples since He believed they were unprepared to assimilate it (John 16:12).

Emphasis in this approach is upon transferring data from the teacher to the pupil, not upon the pupil's ability to discover and make use of this same information on his own. The main concern is over the data and the pupil's absorption of it.

Although the purpose of the Sunday school is to teach God's Word, a mere acquisition of Bible facts falls short of the ultimate objective of observing Christ's commandments (Matthew 28:19,20; 2 Timothy 3:16,17). The teaching of the Scriptures should be aimed at changing pupils spiritually, not programming them like a computer with non-life-related biblical information. When the content of teaching is selected for its relevance and concentrated upon through a variety of pupil-involvement methods, greater understanding of this data results—which is exactly the objective of the content-centered approach!

EMPLOYING CREATIVE METHODS

From the contrasts already discussed, it is obvious that the methods employed in teaching need to be varied and engaging if the teacher is really going to "teach" and the pupil "learn." At one time, standard textbooks on children's education in Sunday school suggested only a handful of methods to be used by the teacher: memorization of Scriptures, storytelling, music and a broad use of visual aids (pictures, flannelgraph, filmstrips, displays).

Pupil workbooks have also been used in the classroom or at home to further assist in the communication of biblical information. Such methods are good, but they limit our teaching effectiveness if we stop here and fail to employ a whole series of methods designed to involve the pupil more directly in Bible study.

Frequently such methods are called "creative," since they allow the pupil to pursue learning goals in ways which are beneficial and expressive to him. Such methods allow him to sense the difficulties and problems in the lives of Bible characters, notice missing information or incidents in stories, find possible explanations about these deficiencies, test them and communicate the results in meaningful ways.

When a third grade child is asked to color in an outlined picture of Jesus speaking to Zacchaeus, for example, he is unable to express his own mental picture and knowledge of this biblical incident. On the other hand, asking him to draw a picture of what he feels is the most important part of this same story will encourage him to understand this event and express it in such a way as to impress its truth more permanently upon his life. Thus our teaching is reinforced.

Here are some other examples of creative methods in which students may learn:

1   Dramatizing a Bible story or making up a story to dramatize which will express how a Bible truth is applied in real life.

2   Building a model Palestinian home, temple or tabernacle as part of a study.

3   Researching a biblical event and writing about it in one's own words.

4   Illustrating through pictures the meaning of a particular Bible passage.

5   Writing the words of a hymn and putting them to music, expressing one's understanding of a series of Bible lessons on God's creation.

6   Making up a different ending to a real life story in order to demonstrate the ability to apply a particular lesson truth.

7   Painting a mural or making a frieze that will show the key sequence in a particular story (a time line on Moses' life or the last few days in Jesus' life, for example).

Some of the basic avenues of creative pupil learning are then seen as: creative writing, dramatization, construction projects, art activities, music activities and research. The wise teacher will seek to use such methods on a regular basis during Sunday school sessions. For a more thorough explanation of these creative methods and how they may be effectively employed in teaching children, you will want to read this book's companion, *Ways To Help Them Learn—Children*, by Barbara J. Bolton.

In summary, such methods have the following advantages:

1   They directly involve the pupil intellectually, physically and emotionally as well as employing most of his five senses.

2 Through them the pupil may express his understanding of the meaning of what is being taught.

3 These pupil expressions give the teacher the opportunity to observe and evaluate his teaching and the pupil's accuracy in comprehending the Bible story or truth being taught.

4 These methods help the pupil to crystallize the Bible content in a concrete form.

5 They are a useful tool in putting the content of an entire series of lessons or unit of study (usually a month long) into a new personal form.

6 They are an effective means through which children can be relating and applying to their own lives the truths being taught (as in the development of a "Daniel and Me" book described later).

IMPROVING THE LEARNING PROCESS

It is evident that the previously mentioned creative teaching methods may frequently be absent from many children's Sunday school classrooms. To teach and minister adequately to children, positive steps toward improved teaching must be taken.

Let us take a close look at the five basic learning steps that are essential to a dynamic learning process in the Sunday school. These are taken from *A Design for Teaching-Learning*[8] and greatly amplified. Notice that such steps are closely related to the characteristics of Jesus' teaching.

LISTENING

Basic to learning in the Sunday school has always been listening. In this case, however, it is used primarily as a point of contact between the pupil and the teacher seeking to initiate the learning process. One of the traditional laws of teaching is that "the pupil must attend with interest to the subject being taught."[9] The Word of God has been, and is, the focus of this step, and the teacher is the amplifier, illustrator and communicator.

Securing the alert listening of the pupil remains a

challenge to today's teacher, since listening alone has less significance in learning today than it had in previous times. With the advent of audiovisual communication tools which often dramatically present subject matter, a child is likely to become restless with a totally audio presentation. When listening is coupled with a visual aid or an activity that engages all of the child's senses, learning is markedly improved. Nevertheless, listening remains an essential task in good teaching. It is considered the initial step in the educational process. Listening may be preceded or stimulated by interest-catching activities such as those you might use in an introduction to the Bible story.

EXPLORING

This second step encompasses a number of significant educational principles. Formerly, Christian educators used the term *acquisition* to signify the process through which the pupil gained knowledge and therefore learned. This term, however, fails to communicate action and pupil activity that is essential to good learning.

On the other hand, the word *exploring* carries the thought of a careful search or investigation of the problem or subject at hand. It tells us something about the child or student; he is an explorer, totally involved in the search for something not yet known or experienced. He is not a passive listener or mere spectator but a very central, active participant in the teaching/learning process.

The word *exploring* also makes us aware that the pupil's interest has been secured and his energies directed toward a relevant, need-fulfilling goal. Learning has become an adventure—something enjoyable and stimulating.

Generally, this enjoyable type of learning environment results from the practice of the following principles suggested in a recent article in the journal *Childhood Education* and slightly adapted here to apply to the Sunday school learning situation.

1 Children are provided with a number of options as far as learning activity is concerned. These may range all the way from researching a Bible story problem or

incident to illustrating through pictures the verse phrases in Psalm 100.

2   Children are able to choose the activity in which they would like to participate. Such a procedure recognizes that children have different interests and talents as well as varying abilities in learning. At times some children may prefer and learn best from art learning projects, while others may profit most from music or research projects.

3   Children can "pose their own problems and determine the manner in which they will pursue them . . . with respect to the materials and activities available" to them.

4   Children can collaborate with their fellow pupils in learning activity. Such cooperation encourages and extends learning, since the children tend to stimulate each other as they progress in the exploration of the subject matter.

5   Children can be trusted by their adult teachers. The principle that guides these teachers is, "I can trust this child until he gives me reason not to, and then I will be more cautious about trusting him in that particular area."

6   Children should have a classroom environment of consistent order and one which minimizes pupil performance comparisons.[10]

The above statements suggest the use of creative methods previously discussed. They will allow for the freedom of choice, varying interests, problem solving and firsthand activity essential to effective learning.

DISCOVERING

At this point in the learning process the "light is turned on" for the pupil. As a result of the listening and exploring processes, guided by the Holy Spirit, he discovers the meaning and value of the particular Scripture content, story or problem for himself. He knows what the Bible says and is soon realizing its implications for his own life.

Discovering truths in the Bible is an exciting experience. It is exciting because it is a personal accomplishment, and the knowledge acquired is a part of God's priceless revelation. Too often the teacher is the one who makes the discoveries in his preparation and then excitedly verbalizes them to his pupils. Why couldn't the joy of discovery also be the child's as he is guided into it by a skilled teacher? How this would stimulate the learning process!

APPROPRIATING

Once the child has discovered the meaning of the Bible lesson, he should be led to think in a personal way about the truths involved. It is essential to good learning that he personally take for himself the meanings and values

THE LEARNING PROCESS

discovered. Certainly this undertaking is an initial step toward observing Bible truths—the result of teaching that Christ desires. A noted psychologist, Dr. Carl Rogers, has claimed that only self-discovered, self-appropriated learning significantly influences behavior.[11]

Greater emphasis should be placed on seeing that our children actually reason out or draw out inferences of a personal nature from the Bible lesson taught during the Sunday school session. Our pupils must understand the Bible as something that makes sense to them now so that they might have confidence in it at the present as well as in the future.

A children's department could accomplish this task by the teachers leading some of the children in making their own "Daniel and Me" booklets, for instance. Each Sunday they would study an aspect of Daniel's exciting life and respond by illustrating Daniel's experience (for example, when he said no to eating food prepared as part of a Babylonian idolotrous ceremony) and a similar experience in which they would also need to respond or behave like Daniel. By the end of the unit of lessons on Daniel, several pages of personal illustrations would compose their booklet showing how they applied and appropriated Daniel's experiences into their own lives.

Other means may also accomplish the task of appropriating. The teacher may just ask a question which would cause the students to draw from the story its meaning to their own lives. ("What does our Bible story mean to you, Sharon?") A real childhood problem may also be posed for the children to solve on the basis of the lesson truth. Bill loved baseball and was playing the last inning when he realized that it was past dinner time. He knew his parents would be waiting for him but he did not want to leave the game. What should he do? Using an open-end story for the children to complete may also accomplish the same purpose. For example, Steve asked Carol if he could copy her homework and Carol decided . . . because. . . .

Personally appropriating the Bible lesson truth is an important level of learning for each child. It is then that he is able to see plainly its meaning for his own life and behavior. Therefore, he knows what God expects of him in situations related to this truth. The end of the learning process has not been reached, however, since the pupil has not yet put the lesson truth to use in his actual experience.

ASSUMING RESPONSIBILITY

This is the crown of the learning process, the place where the previous tasks—listening, exploring and appropriating—culminate. This is where God's truth actually changes and molds a child's thinking and behavior. Once this has occurred, the child can be said to have really learned or experienced the lesson truth taught.

It is apparent that this final learning task is most important. It is at this point that our efforts as teachers to effectively communicate God's truth should result in changed lives. Our children must see the necessity of taking certain actions on the basis of what has been taught. They need to see clearly the actions necessitated by the study and be led into assuming responsibility for them.

The whole process of human understanding and learning is summed up in these learning steps. They are not simply activities in which pupils are to be engaged but are inseparably bound up with Christian teaching goals and objectives.[12] Guiding our children into and through these tasks should greatly encourage their spiritual development, causing them to constantly observe Christ's commandments and put them into practice daily.

FOOTNOTES

CHAPTER 2

1 · Lois E. LeBar, *Education That Is Christian* (Westwood, N.J.: Fleming H. Revell Co., 1958), pp. 82-85.

2 · Cornelius Jaarsma, *Human Development, Learning and Teaching* (Grand Rapids: Wm. B. Eerdmans Publishing Co., 1959), p. 217.

3 · Bonnidell Clouse, "Psychosocial Origins of Stability in the Christian Faith," *Christianity Today,* September 25, 1970, pp. 12-14.

4 · Eda J. LeShan, *The Conspiracy Against Childhood* (New York: Atheneum, 1967), p. 143.

5 · Betty L. Broman, "Too Much Shushing—Let Children Talk," *Childhood Education,* vol. 46, no. 3, December 1969, pp. 132-134.

6 · Joseph Bayly, *Christian Education Trends* (Elgin, Ill.: David C. Cook Publishing Co., 1969), p. 4.

7 · Jack R. Frymier, *Learning Centers: Children on Their Own* (Washington D.C.: The Association for Childhood Education International, 1970), pp. 8-9.

8 · Cooperative Curriculum Project, *A Design for Teaching-Learning* (St. Louis: Bethany Press, 1967), p. 33.

9 · John Milton Gregory, *The Seven Laws of Teaching,* Revised Edition (Grand Rapids: Baker Book House, 1962), p. 24.

10 · Roland S. Barth, "When Children Enjoy School," *Childhood Education,* January 1970, pp. 196-198.

11 · Virginia Ramey MollenKott, "Teachers, Students and Self-fishness," *Christianity Today,* April 24, 1970, p. 15.

12 · C. Campbell Wyckoff, *Theory and Design of Christian Education Curriculum* (Philadelphia: The Westminster Press, 1961), pp. 151-153.

MAKING SUNDAY MORNING COUNT

Ten year old Todd ran to his Sunday school room. It was 9:20 A.M., and his weekly hour of formal Bible instruction was about to begin. He bounded into the room to find two other pupils—his friend David and a visitor. There was no teacher in sight, so he moved to the old upright piano and pounded on it. Five minutes later Mrs. Cavender, the superintendent, hurried into the room, loaded down with her supplies. At her suggestion Todd and the other two children placed the songbooks on every other chair. The secretary arrived, registered the visitors and began her normal record keeping.

In ten minutes the opening exercises began with the singing of a familiar chorus. The children didn't sing loudly enough, so Mrs. Cavender urged them all to "run through it again." After the prayer and during the third song, Chet Brown, Todd's teacher arrived. With some jostling for seats, Todd managed to sit by his collegiate teacher. This movement was all to the tune of "Onward Christian Soldiers!"

Mrs. Cavender spent time talking about the church's building program and the need for funds. Following the offering three students shared their birthdates, and the children all sang "Happy Birthday." Mrs. Cavender talked about the "second birthday" that children must have and called on Charlotte to recite John 3:16 and 17. She then mentioned that it was late and rushed the children and their teachers to their classrooms. The children raced for the seats nearest the windows.

Todd's teacher had two classes this morning; one of

the teachers failed to arrive, for some unknown reason. Mr. Brown let the children share some of their experiences of the past week and welcomed Ross and Stephen, who hadn't been present for several Sundays. ("Where have you boys been all these weeks?")

The Bible story was about Moses. Only three pupils had the Old Testament portion of the Scriptures, so everyone tried to follow along using the Bibles available and struggled through the reading of the 21 verses. Then Mr. Brown explained some of the key parts of the story and showed a picture of Moses holding the "stone commandments." ("Don't they look heavy?") Mr. Brown told how he was spanked by his dad when he didn't obey his commandments and how it is the same with God's children when they fail to obey His teachings.

All of the pupils practiced saying the memory verse, "Thou shalt not make unto thee any graven image . . ., Thou shalt not bow down thyself to them . . .," and were soon busy answering the questions and filling in the blanks in their workbooks. (Todd had done his lesson at home.) Three students had lost or didn't bring their workbooks, so they shared the teacher's copy. Two pupils were still struggling over the first few items on the page, which were obviously above their reading ability level, when Mr. Brown called it quits and said, "Good-bye until next week." As the teacher hurried off to choir, Todd and his friends raced each other to the drinking fountain. Another hour in Sunday school was now history.

WHAT'S WRONG HERE?

You who have taught in children's Sunday school departments probably recognize portions of the above teaching situation as all too real. What would you say were the weaknesses of this 60 minute session? Were there any strong points? Having a room in which to meet, songs to sing, Bibles to read, teachers to teach and pupils to learn are all fundamental to Christian education.

These factors alone, however, will not teach children to live according to the precepts of God's Word. You probably noticed the following weaknesses in our hypothetical Sunday school hour (and perhaps in some actual Sunday school sessions in which you have participated):

1 No teacher was on hand for the children who arrived early. Not only was potential teaching time wasted, but a discipline problem was created.

2 Some teachers were late, and others were absent without substitutes to replace them. Do you think this situation might cause the children to conclude that Sunday school attendance is not important?

3 The assembly period did not relate to the Bible story and lesson aim. Aside from fellowship, this period contributed almost nothing to the hour.

4 Disorder, rather than discipline, prevailed much of the time. Having a teacher ready with an activity for the first children to arrive and dismissing the children by classes instead of en masse would be two simple and obvious remedies.

5 Mr. Brown did not seem to know what the aim of his lesson was.

6 There was not a variety of activities to fit the children's different abilities and interests nor to allow for exploration, discovery, real-life application or creative expression.

Because of weaknesses such as these, the Sunday school hour is often wasted.

Teachers and leaders should think of "total session" teaching and learning. By this term is meant that virtually everything that is done during the Sunday school assembly period and the class period should be directed toward fulfilling the lesson aim for that Sunday. Little side trips which receive undue emphasis will divert the children's attention from the lesson elements which emphasize the spiritual aim. As you plan and teach, constantly keep in mind the one central truth you wish the children to learn each Sunday.

MAKING MORE OF THE TIME

Many Christian educators have been unhappy with the hour-long Sunday school because they have felt that it just couldn't carry the educational load. Trying to teach well in only 40 to 50 hours a year has been called an impossible dream.

Behind this criticism has been the assumption, as Locke E. Bowman puts it, ". . . that the more time a teacher has with his pupils, the better." The root issue, however, goes unexamined: "How much can you do with an hour?"[1] Is the church effectively using the 60 minutes it already has? What assurance do we have that additional time will be useful and productive?

According to Bowman, one-third to one-half of every Sunday school hour in the typical church is wasted.[2] A survey has shown that the average teaching time is only 29 minutes.

The lament over the shortness of the Sunday school hour is probably without secure foundation, concludes Bowman. With improved teaching methods and growing educational technology, an hour has overwhelming potential.[3] These facts should not lead us to conclude that more time for Sunday school is not needed, but rather that the time we do have is often ill used.

SIXTY PLUS FIFTEEN

In view of the growing challenge of teaching today's children, giving some additional time for this purpose would certainly be helpful. Not only do our children live in a very secular culture, but growing family mobility may keep them from attending Sunday school with regularity. When the children are present, you want to make a greater impact upon their lives, and extending the teaching hour by 10 or 15 minutes will help you to do so.

Creative Bible teaching methods require more time, since the pupils are directly involved. They are searching out God's Word for themselves and expressing their discoveries in various concrete forms. The usual elements of a Sunday school hour—the Bible story, memory work and music—are still very much a part of a good learning experience for children. With the addition of the creative learning activities, teachers may feel pressed for time, even when efforts have been made to trim any non-essentials from the teaching period.

Pastors, directors of Christian education and Sunday school superintendents are urged to seriously consider the lengthening of their Sunday school hour by 15 minutes. Some churches already have a 75 minute Sunday school session. Not only does this additional time benefit teaching, but it has the potential of adding 13 more hours of Christian education to the normal 52 hours available in the Sunday school program. This time is equivalent to an extra quarter each year! Think of the potential a fifth quarter has in teaching your children.

| **TRADITIONAL SESSION** | **60** minutes | |
| **IDEAL SESSION** | **75** minutes | (Totaling one extra quarter a year!) |

Whatever the allotted time period is for your Sunday school, your primary concern is to use the whole hour, or hour and 15 minutes, to the fullest in accomplishing the quality Bible teaching and learning described in chapter 2. We are spiritually obligated to redeem the time available to serve Christ, for once a moment and opportunity have been spent, they may never be spent again. An organized plan for each minute will be a great help in making the best use of the time you have to teach your pupils.

FAMILIAR TIME SCHEDULES

Sunday school curriculum publishers have always recommended a particular time and activity schedule for children's departments and classes to follow. Most churches have been guided by these recommended schedules, while some have, out of necessity, adjusted them to fit their particular circumstances.

There have been usually two basic parts to these schedules: a department or assembly worship period (15 to 20 minutes in length) and an individual class teaching period (40 to 45 minutes). These two periods may or may not have had a close relationship as far as teaching content is concerned. The department superintendent led the worship time, which included music, prayer, the offering, recognition of visitors and certain promotional emphases. The teachers led their classes in reviewing past lessons, telling the Bible story, practicing the memory verses and possibly allowing time for the pupil lesson books to be checked and/or completed.

In the above pattern there was the tendency for the pupil to take a passive, listening role rather than one which demanded the use of all of his learning capabilities. Studies have demonstrated that a pupil listens only one-fifth of the time to a teacher's verbal presentation. The other four-fifths of his time is spent in a variety of ways to escape boredom: inspecting the room, doodling or drawing pictures, or thinking about other events which remind him of this situation.[4]

FIVE FACTORS BEHIND A NEW PLAN AND SCHEDULE

If we are really to redeem the time in Sunday school for life-changing teaching, we must get our pupils actively involved in learning. The Sunday school schedule presented in this book, rather than having the teacher simply tell the pupils everything, will guide them through creative methods to discover and appropriate Bible truths. Five organizational factors are involved in this schedule.

TOTAL SESSION TEACHING

Each minute of your Sunday school session should contribute to the lesson aim for that week. Every part of your plan for the morning should emphasize the specific purpose of the lesson.

Being "total session minded" in your teaching will

have the following advantages: 1) It will conserve the teaching time by eliminating material not related to the specific aim of the lesson; 2) It will direct and unify the entire class and assembly group teaching thrust according to the specified lesson aim; 3) It will provide for the department superintendent and the teachers a controlling purpose and guideline for their work in the various groupings within the department session; 4) It will result in more permanent learning for the pupils due to the increased concentration on the lesson material and aim in both the class, assembly and activity groups.

UNIT-CENTERED TEACHING

A unit consists of a series of lessons on from three to five Sundays centered on one theme and purpose. Every Sunday session expands on this central theme and contributes to the unit purpose.

Unit teaching has the following advantages: 1) The lessons are all related and emphasize one central aim, thereby unifying the teaching-learning emphasis; 2) It directs the teaching process toward fulfilling basic spiritual objectives. Units of Bible study are based upon the needs of children in a particular age group; 3) It allows for a continuation of theme which is commensurate with the interest of a student: 4) It provides time for pupil research—exploring and discovering Bible information through small group activities with filmstrips, books, displays and pictures. Interviews and field trips may even be conducted during the week and reported on during the Sunday session; 5) It emphasizes the pupils' learning experiences rather than the teachers'. The unit approach is directed toward helping the pupil actually experience Bible truths rather than simply having the truths presented by the teacher.[5]

BIBLE LEARNING ACTIVITIES

Children learn best when they are intellectually and physically active. A variety of creative learning activities should be used to involve the pupil purposefully in Bible study. These creative activities generally require mental and physical participation (creative writing, dramatization, construction projects, art and music activities) and should always contribute directly to the aim of a lesson or unit.

There are two lengths of time involved in Bible learning activities, weekly and by the unit. Weekly activities are those which begin and end in a single Sunday school session. Unit activities are continuing in nature; they are more involved and demand more time. Your pupils work on these activities in gradual steps over the period of the unit of study, generally from three to five Sundays long. Dramatizing a Bible story or writing a letter expressing how a Bible character felt when he faced an important decision might be suitable activities to complete in one session. Activities requiring a whole unit might include painting a mural or making a booklet about Bible commands and ways they can help children make right decisions. There is a world of projects which can be done in either the weekly or unit activities.

There are three types and purposes of learning activities: 1) Those that are used primarily to arouse interest or capture attention; 2) Those that help children find facts or discover information; and 3) Those designed to encourage children to express knowledge, understanding or feelings.[6] Both the weekly and unit activities will be designed to fulfill at least one of the above purposes.

PUPIL CHOICE AND PLANNING

Many of your pupils do not function according to their capabilities, since they lack learning motivation. One principle of leadership is that ". . . people support only what they help to create."[7] This statement is clearly relevant to the teaching-learning process.

Our children are frequently unmotivated toward meaningful and enjoyable participation in our teaching plans, since they never helped to make the plans. This built-in resistance toward accepting what they have not helped to create may express itself in a number of ways, ranging from indifference and boredom to misbehavior. You have seen these pupil attitudes but may have failed to consider the root cause to be anything more than, "It's the age" or "Children are certainly difficult to teach nowadays."

Your pupils' enjoyment and subsequent motivation in Bible study will be significantly improved if they are given a choice in determining the learning activities in which they will be engaged. Choices of activities are made from a restricted range of alternatives related to the theme and aim of the Bible study unit.

The children will be further motivated when you give them the freedom to plan out the details of the learning activity. Under your guidance the activity is broken into logical working parts and steps of completion. Each child selects one or more of the parts as his responsibility. Such peer group collaboration adds further enjoyment and impetus to the learning process.

In allowing for both pupil choice and pupil planning in the teaching schedule, you simultaneously put into practice the processes inherent in the key learning tasks—listening, exploring, discovering, appropriating and assuming responsibility. Research has shown that when the learner is activated through such processes, learning motivation is greatly increased.[8]

VARIED PUPIL GROUPINGS

The pupil groupings will continue the pattern of the permanent class group and the department group. In addition to these groups, there will be another small, temporary grouping of pupils that will be formed at the beginning of each unit to carry out the learning activities. On the first Sunday of the unit in the large group time, children will choose the learning activity in which they wish to participate. At the conclusion of either the entire unit or the weekly activities these temporary pupil groups will be dissolved.

Some children may choose to work on weekly activities, those that can be completed within the Sunday school time on any given Sunday. Others, especially older children with a longer interest span, may choose an activity which will be carried out through the entire unit. Thus, each pupil has the option to participate in whatever form of activity that suits his interest and needs at that time.

Men and women teachers will continue to teach the Bible lesson to their assigned class of pupils but will also assume the leadership of one of the temporary activity learning groups. Each activity group is likely to include children from most of the department's classes. Thus, both boys and girls will work together in the activity groups. The tendency for the pupils to group themselves according to sex will be noticeable in the fifth and sixth grades and should not be encouraged or discouraged. It is simply a natural developmental stage through which older children must pass (with a little grace, we hope).

Not only will these activity groups provide creative learning experiences for the pupils, but they will also give the children some intimate contact and exposure with other adult Christian personalities. Under the former plan children tended to build a personal relationship with their class teacher only. Now their lives will be touched by each adult teacher, and the opportunities to learn through identification and imitation of adult models will be increased. Furthermore, in some cases, someone other than a pupil's class teacher may be able to minister more effectively to him. A team teaching relationship is fostered in this arrangement.

On the last Sunday of some units the children will have the opportunity to share in the department group their learning experiences and knowledge gained through participation in the activity groups. This time of actually having the children share is not necessary for every unit. The curriculum will suggest other methods for evaluating learning that are equally as effective. This procedure may take some additional time but will be an excellent way to reinforce the unit study through the pupils' expression of their learning experiences. The anticipation of this time will tend to stimulate interest and enthusiasm in the activity groups while the unit study is in process.

NEW SCHEDULES

In an effort to employ the educational factors discussed, thus improving the quality of Christian education, new Sunday school time schedules are recommended.

PLAN A

HOW TO USE YOUR TOTAL SESSION TEACHING TIME

BIBLE STUDY	BIBLE SHARING/ PLANNING	BIBLE LEARNING ACTIVITIES
This diagram represents the first block of time for the Sunday school period. It includes all the material to be used in the permanent class grouping. When the child arrives, he begins working on an activity that builds readiness for Bible learning. He then listens to the Bible story and thinks through ways of applying to his own life the truths he learned from God's Word.	This diagram represents the time when all the children in the department are together in a large group. Normally it will be the second time block in the Sunday school hour. All the children share together in worship and other large group activities. Then each child selects the Bible learning activity he wants to work on during the third block of time.	This diagram represents the block of time which normally is the last portion of the Sunday school period. Children are divided into small nonpermanent groups, according to the activities they choose to work on. A teacher leads each activity. Note that at this time the teacher does not work with his own class group, but rather with the children who choose the activity he is leading.

If you have 75 minutes

25-35 minutes	up to 15 minutes	20-25 minutes

If you have 60 minutes

25-30 minutes	up to 10 minutes	20 minutes

Note: For review purposes of each unit, the last two blocks of time can be reversed —children go directly from class time to their Bible learning activities; then all could meet together for large group time. This would allow children to complete their Bible learning activities (small groups) and then to share what they learned during the unit (large group).

THREE TIME PERIODS

Reference was made earlier to three types of teaching groups: one large group and two small groups. Each of these groups takes up a portion of the Sunday school session. Each of these time periods is, of necessity, shorter than those two larger time periods (assembly and class) found in the former schedules for children's departments.

These three periods are time blocks which can be arranged in different ways (Plan A). In the 75-minute Sunday school session, the large group, containing all of the classes, would last for an average of 10 to 15 minutes. The permanent class groups, where the Bible story is taught, would last for 25 to 35 minutes. The Bible learning activity groups would continue for a duration of 20 to 25 minutes.

BASIC SCHEDULE

The recommended schedule (Plan A) includes a 75-minute session which begins with the small class group, moves to the large assembly group and then to the activity group.

On the last Sunday of the unit the schedule will be changed to allow for a culmination of the unit and the learning activities. Once again the small class group will start the Sunday session, but at the completion of this period the children will move to their temporary Bible learning activity groups rather than to the large group. The children will be led to complete their activities and plan for sharing and evaluating them in the larger assembly period which follows.

The advantages of this schedule are as follows:

1   The session begins with the foundation of the Bible story taught on a small, teacher-to-pupil basis. This procedure facilitates Bible lesson application, since the teacher knows the needs of his own pupils. Such a plan also helps develop the remaining assembly and activity group periods, since they will build upon the Bible information studied in the classes.

2   The department group, falling in the middle of the session, provides both group worship and a logical

platform for transition from the permanent class groups to the temporary activity groups. On the first Sunday the department superintendent introduces the unit study and leads the children in choosing a learning activity that interests them most. In the weeks that follow the superintendent serves as an educational catalyst, seeking to bring the unit study to a successful conclusion through his personal encouragement and unifying efforts during the large group times. This is especially true on the last Sunday of the unit as the children share their Bible learning activities.

3 The more active time block, the Bible learning activity portion, is placed at the end of the session when the children are most likely to be restless and inattentive

ADVANTAGES OF USING TOTAL SESSION TEACHING

BIBLE STUDY (permanent class groups)	BIBLE SHARING/ PLANNING (department group)	BIBLE LEARNING ACTIVITIES (small temporary groups)
1 Session begins with the foundation of the Bible story taught on a small personal teacher-to-pupil basis. Remainder of period builds on this. 2 Permanent teacher can make Bible lesson application more personal since he knows better the needs of his small group. 3 Child identifies with one adult. 4 Small, permanent group insures child of the individual attention, concern, love and help he needs. 5 Permanent teacher can do more thorough job of home visitation and contacts.	1 Child learns to share in corporate worship experiences. 2 Child has opportunity to see total picture of which his small group is a part. Superintendent can unify and encourage the work of the small groups. 3 Child can choose Bible learning activity of interest to him—increasing motivation and learning. 4 At culmination of unit, child can share with others what he learned, and learn from seeing and hearing what others share.	1 Child can work with a peer group of his choice. 2 Child can participate in activity that interests him, which increases his motivation. 3 Child has opportunity to interact with other adults besides his class teacher (in some cases they may be able to minister more effectively to him). 4 This more active time block comes at the end of the session, when children need a more engaging activity than listening.

and in need of something more engaging and active than listening.

4 The changes in approach to teaching the pupil and the two occasions of movement from the class group to the assembly group and then to the activity group are in keeping with a grade school child's active physical and intellectual makeup and should tend to reduce boredom and misbehavior.

ALTERNATE SCHEDULES

Two other schedules are offered here to those churches which can provide a 60-minute session but not a 75-minute instruction period. The first alternate schedule differs only in time allotted to each session as shown in Plan A. The class group is shortened to 25 to 30 minutes, the large group to 10 minutes, and the activity group to 20.

The second alternate schedule (Plan B) is a rearrangement of the time blocks. The large group comes toward the end of the session and serves to unify and conclude the instruction period. The children do

PLAN B

ANOTHER WAY OF USING THE LESSON MATERIAL

BIBLE STUDY/BIBLE LEARNING ACTIVITIES 40 minutes (permanent class group)	BIBLE SHARING 15-20 minutes (department group)
Teacher uses suggestions in Bible Study time and chooses one Bible learning activity for his entire class to take part in.	Department Superintendent adapts material from Bible Sharing/Planning section. Music and conversation are thus an outgrowth and/or expression of what was learned in class time. Note that it will not be necessary to allow for planning and choosing Bible learning activities when material is arranged in this way.

not move to an activity group but remain in their permanent class with their assigned teacher to participate in a Bible learning activity. The teacher may choose this activity or allow the children the freedom to choose the activity which the majority prefers.

The second alternate schedule will keep all unit sessions in the same order throughout the unit. On the last Sunday of the unit, however, the Bible learning activity time will be shortened by five minutes, and this added time will be used in the department period. This will allow additional time for sharing the activities and bringing the unit to a successful conclusion.

PROVISION FOR DIVERSITY

There may be occasions when the department superintendent will want to adjust the time allotted for the various periods in the basic and first alternate schedules. For instance, during the second and third Sundays of a unit, after the study has been introduced and prior to its conclusion, the large group time could be shortened to allow a few additional minutes for either the class or activity study groups. More group time is usually needed on the first Sunday, since the children are choosing learning activities, and on the last Sunday, as the children share and discuss these activities and the knowledge they have acquired.

Some time may also be conserved by conducting the large group time as the children are in their class groups sitting around their study tables. This arrangement is only possible, however, when the children are being taught in an open department room where they can be in full view of the department superintendent.

If there is a carpeted room or large floor rug, the children could be asked to come from their study areas and sit on the floor while the department session is conducted. Time consumed in rearranging chairs for the assembly period could be saved for small group study purposes.

This particular arrangement may also be suitable for the traditional room which has small classrooms and an assembly area. If there is a shortage of chairs, time may be wasted in moving them back and forth from the

SELECT THE PLAN THAT IS BEST FOR YOU

Find on the chart below the organizational plan that is most similar to the one you are now using. Then consider what changes you will want to make to move toward using Plan A when it is possible in your Sunday school. In the meantime, you can adapt your Sunday school material to follow Plan B. Your Sunday school material can be used in any of the following ways:

Organization of Department	Plan to Use	How to Use It
Closely-graded Department (classes are all from the same grade)	Plan A or Plan B	Use Plan A as suggested. If you have limited time, use Plan B as suggested.
Group-graded Department (classes are from more than one grade)	Plan A or Plan B	If classes from two grades must be combined in one department, use Plan A as suggested. Cycle the curriculum over a two-year period: use the curriculum for one grade one year and the curriculum for the other grade the next year. (Do not cycle more than two grades.) If at all possible, do not combine first grade with any other grade because first graders are just learning to read and write. If more than two grades must be temporarily combined in one department, use Plan B as follows: Each class meets separately by grade level (use Bible Study/Bible Learning Activity sections of curriculum during class time). Then classes combine for worship and use thematic worship services. ("Primaries Worship" for grades 1-3, and "Worship Programs for Juniors" for grades 4-6, published by G/L Publications, are available from your church supplier.)
Single-grade class (one class group stays together for entire period)	Plan A or Plan B	Use sequence suggested in Plan A, but conduct Bible Sharing/Planning activities in your class. If you have an assistant, you can provide two Bible learning activities and let children choose which activity they want to work on. If you are limited by time, use sequence suggested in Plan B, but conduct Bible Sharing activities in your class.

classrooms to the assembly room and then back to the classrooms.

Since each church will have individual needs, remember that these sessions are designed to be flexible within the framework of individual Sunday school programs. Adjustments can easily be made in the curriculum suggestions to suit each need. Those involved in the Sunday school program should evaluate their individual situations and adjust to suit.

In summary, there are four recommendations for making Sunday morning count:

1   Use wisely the time available for Sunday school instruction by directing all teaching toward the lesson aim and by using more creative teaching methods.

2   Seriously consider extending the Sunday school hour by 15 minutes to provide additional time for effective teaching and learning.

3   Realize the importance of the five factors (pp. 44-48) behind the new plan and see that their educational advantages are capitalized upon.

4   Adopt the basic time schedule, or, if need be, one of the alternate schedules to provide a workable framework for the Sunday school session.

FOOTNOTES

CHAPTER 3

1 · Locke E. Bowman, Jr., *Straight Talk About Teaching in Today's Church* (Philadelphia: Westminster Press, 1968), pp. 90-94.

2 · Bowman, *Straight Talk About Teaching in Today's Church*, p. 97.

3 · Bowman, *Straight Talk About Teaching in Today's Church*, p. 97.

4 · B. F. Jackson, Jr., ed., *Communication: Learning for Churchmen, Vol. 1* (Nashville: Abingdon Press, 1968), p. 176.

5 · Delores Baker and Elsie Rives, *Teaching the Bible to Primaries* (Nashville: Convention Press, 1964), pp. 87-89.

6 · Robert A. Hary, *Children in Church Training* (Nashville: Convention Press, 1969), p. 77.

7 · Bruce Larson, *No Longer Strangers* (Waco: Word Books, 1971), p. 23.

8 · Jackson, *Communication: Learning for Churchmen*, p. 161.

CHAPTER FOUR

ORGANIZE TO ENCOURAGE LEARNING

It took someone with a keen management eye to see
the solution to Moses' problem. From morning until night
he singlehandedly judged the affairs of all the tribes of
Israel. Jethro had such managerial qualifications. Although a rural priest, he possessed the ability and insight
of a top business executive. Possibly he acquired these
skills through the successful management of not only
his priestly affairs but of his family and livestock interests
as well. The management of men and work was an area
in which he apparently had few equals. Moses had much
respect for Jethro and valued his presence (Exodus
18:7-27).

Jethro wisely advised Moses to follow two procedures:
teach the Israelites some basic life and work laws and
recruit able administrative assistants to share his responsibilities in governing the people.

Related to these procedures was a vast and detailed
organizational plan. The families of all twelve Israelite
tribes were to be divided into groups of thousands,
hundreds, fifties and tens. This division into the smallest
possible groups of people was at the heart of this plan's
potential success. Over each group Moses would place
one of his administrative assistants. They would be responsible for the affairs of the people within their groups,
and only matters of large significance would be referred
to Moses. This division of responsibility and labor was
promised to bring about greater efficiency in governing
God's people. "If thou shalt do this thing . . . then thou

shalt be able to endure, and all this people shall also go to their place in peace."[1]

Although organizational matters have sometimes been given a place of lesser spiritual significance in the work of the church, they do have a definite part in the work of reaching and teaching people for Christ. Throughout the history of the Sunday school, good organization has proved essential for growth and quality teaching.

GRADING—BASIS OF ORGANIZATION

An effective leader in Sunday school work, Henrietta Mears, once said, "Ninety percent of failure is lack of organization." Inherent in her Sunday school organization was the division of pupils of various ages into small, manageable and teachable groups. She knew the most logical plan for such division was by pupil age or grade. Thus, early in her ministry as Director of Christian Education at the famed First Presbyterian Church of Hollywood (California), she set out to develop a separate department for each age. Frequently she was heard saying, "God closely graded children; I didn't." Her dream was a Sunday school growing to the place where it provided a department corresponding with each public school elementary grade, first through sixth grades, with more adequate teaching and learning possible at each stage of pupil development.

Of crucial importance to this proven approach in education is the value of small teaching groups. At times Jesus instructed large groups of people, but the great majority of His teaching experiences were in small groups, including some 57 person-to-person encounters.[2] Little wonder that He was called "teacher," or its equivalent, almost one hundred times.[3] It was in these small groups that people most effectively learned of their needs and of the Saviour's purposes, promises and plans for their lives.

The advantages of organizing children into teaching groups of five to eight pupils are numerous:

1 Small groups make it easier for pupils to feel socially a part of the group. Children are able to share

with one another, and out of this sharing will come mutual understanding and acceptance.

2 Small groups provide a context in which teachers may more easily acquaint themselves with their pupils' backgrounds, needs and interests, so they will be more able to meet individual needs when they teach.

3 Small groups assist in the development of wholesome teacher-pupil relationships so basic to a good learning environment.

4 Small groups make it possible for pupils to determine and plan group activities together and thereby encourage maximum contributions to such activities.

5 Small groups make easier the evaluation and review of group progress by teacher and pupils.

6 Small groups are the ideal context for teaching which employs creative methods and for learning which encourages the process of listening, exploring, discovering, appropriating and assuming responsibility.

7 Small groups tend to lessen the potential for discipline problems and make the teaching-learning process more manageable for the teacher.

8 Small groups encourage numerical growth, since both members and visitors are able to be personally involved and are given the teacher's personal attention.

9 Small groups encourage spiritual growth in the pupils, since they have a closer and more personal relationship with their Bible teachers than they could possibly have in a larger group.

GRADING—BASIS OF GROWTH

It is a common practice in the majority of Sunday schools to group several grades of children together into one department. Generally, the first three grades compose the first group, and the fourth, fifth and sixth grades the other. Whenever two or more grades are grouped together into a department, the department is what we term "group graded."

Some Sunday schools group children into six separate grade level departments. These departments are termed "closely graded." The most effective learning plan is to closely grade your children in the learning group.

Many churches do not have enough children, however, to warrant the organization of six grade level departments, so they must group grade. In this case one of two curriculum plans will be followed in order to preserve the value of total session teaching discussed in chapter 3.

First, you may cycle closely graded curriculum by using one grade level of curriculum for the entire department for one year and a following grade level's for the next year. It is not recommended that you cycle over more than a two-year grade span. Cycling is appropriate between any two-year combination of grades except first grade which should remain separate whenever possible because of reading aptitude at that age.

An alternate plan for the Sunday school which must group grade their pupils includes the organization of "single-grade classes" which can use closely graded literature almost entirely as designed. Single-graded classes are what their name implies; they are composed of one grade level of children and they operate independently of other classes during the entire Sunday school session. Each teacher leads his small class group in the Bible lesson, worship experience and Bible learning activities. Such curriculum cycling may also be employed when small class groups must be composed of two grades of pupils. Generally, teachers will follow the second alternate schedule explained in chapter 3, with the assembly period the only exclusion. Music experiences may be easily provided through the use of a phonograph, cassette tapes and appropriate records or through the use of an Autoharp.

Once such single-grade classes exceed eight attending pupils, they should be divided. Generally, when both classes begin to average more than 12 pupils combined, a department should be created composed of these two classes (if space and teachers are available).

FACTORS IN GRADING

Correct grading encourages growth. However, three factors must be kept in mind to assure good growth procedures.

ATTENDANCE

The first factor to consider is the number of children attending your Sunday school. A children's department should consist of no more than 30 pupils. Classes within a department should contain no more than 5 to 8 children.

With a minimum number of 12 pupils, a children's department may be organized and led by a department superintendent and two teachers.

Grades		Number of Pupils
Dept.	1	20
Dept.	2	15
Dept.	3	9
	4	8
Dept.	5	7
	6	10

If the number of children at each of the six grade levels is uneven, grouping them into separate departments for each grade may be impractical. A single department for the larger grade groups and combining two of the smaller groups into one department would solve the problem. For example, if you have 20 first graders, 15 second graders, 9 third graders, 8 fourth and 7 fifth graders and 10 sixth graders, you might provide a department for the first graders, one for the second, one for the third and fourth graders, and another for the fifth and sixth graders—a total of four department groupings.

AVAILABLE SPACE AND EQUIPMENT

The second factor that influences the grading of children into manageable teaching units is the availability of space and equipment. After you determine the number of departments needed to care adequately for your children, you will want to take an inventory of the rooms being used for the Sunday school.

Your church may be allocating only two rooms for children when four are needed. Often an adult or youth class may be moved to another location in the church or an adjacent building to provide the space needed.

As space is made available for new groups of children, some attention must be given to needed equipment. Chapter 6 deals thoroughly with inexpensive equipment that a church may use to provide a good learning environment for children. If you wish, turn to chapter 6 and scan equipment lists for grades one through six.

AVAILABLE LEADERSHIP

Of great importance is the amount of leadership available and needed to staff the children's departments. New department groupings can function adequately only when a sufficient teaching staff is provided.

There should be a teacher for every five to eight pupils in attendance. According to this ratio, you should begin planning toward a new department when you are using five teachers, considering an average of six pupils per class. This situation would in turn necessitate the recruitment of another department superintendent, who may come from the ranks of those already teaching.

An inventory of potential teachers in the church is one of the first steps to be taken. Contacting these prospects in a personal, face-to-face way will bring about the best results. They should be fully informed of their duties, of how teaching is accomplished in your departments and of the average time required to fill the role successfully. Observation of an actual Sunday school session should be suggested to acquaint these individuals with your teaching plan. Training opportunities should also be shared. Be certain to point out the personal growth in teaching, both for the Sunday school students and for the teacher's own life.

Once you have determined the department groupings needed, located the additional room and equipment and recruited the leadership, your children's ministry can be enlarged. These three factors compose the major considerations in grouping your children in Sunday school.

PATTERNS FOR GROUPING AND GRADING

Group your children into departments according to one of the following organizational patterns, depending upon the size of your children's attendance and the available space and leadership.

CLOSELY GRADED CLASSES

In churches where the children's attendance is small, it might be wise to dispense with the department system altogether and merely use classes as independent groups during the Sunday school session (Diagram 1). *A class consists of one teacher and no more than 5 to 8 pupils attending.* Each class would then be closely graded. The closely graded class should be formed into a department when the number of attending children is 12 or more and staff and space are available (Diagram 2). The closely graded curriculum would adapt itself easily to these classes.

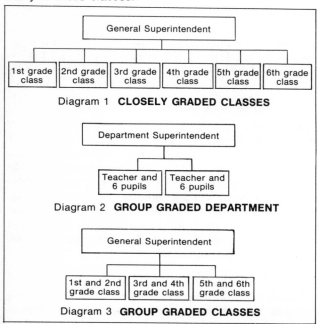

Diagram 1 **CLOSELY GRADED CLASSES**

Diagram 2 **GROUP GRADED DEPARTMENT**

Diagram 3 **GROUP GRADED CLASSES**

GROUP GRADED CLASSES

An alternative to closely graded classes is group graded classes, combining no more than two consecutive grades of children (Diagram 3). For example, if there is a minimum number of both third and fourth graders, combining the two classes to form a group graded class composed of both groups could be functional. The same formation might apply equally as well to the first and second graders or the fifth and sixth graders. The closely graded curriculum would then be cycled to adapt to the classes which would be formed.

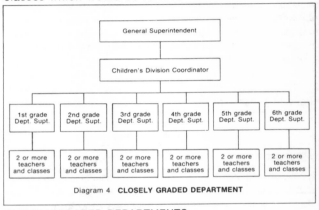

Diagram 4 **CLOSELY GRADED DEPARTMENT**

CLOSELY GRADED DEPARTMENTS

A department consists of a minimum of 12 and maximum of 30 pupils, from 2 to 5 teachers, and a department superintendent. When an individual class reaches an attendance of 12 pupils, it is time to form that class into a department. A closely graded department would then consist of at least two classes (and, of course, at least two teachers), and a department superintendent (Diagram 4). When a department reaches an attendance of 30 pupils, we recommend that it be divided once more to provide two departments.

GROUP GRADED DEPARTMENTS

If two consecutive age groups have combined classes with over 12 attending pupils, a group graded department system may be formed (Diagram 5). In this case, for example, with 7 first graders and 6 second graders, a group graded department composed of these two classes would total 13 pupils. The same arrangement might work efficiently for third and fourth graders and fifth and sixth graders. Again, the curriculum may be adapted to this group graded situation by cycling it over a two-year period.

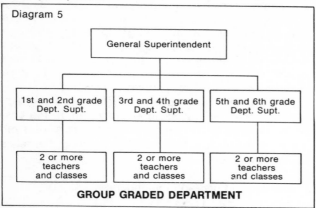

Diagram 5

General Superintendent

1st and 2nd grade Dept. Supt.

3rd and 4th grade Dept. Supt.

5th and 6th grade Dept. Supt.

2 or more teachers and classes

2 or more teachers and classes

2 or more teachers and classes

GROUP GRADED DEPARTMENT

ASSEMBLY TIME WITH CLASSES FOLLOWING

Some churches may wish to continue the opening assembly time in their Sunday schools with multiple grades attending. In this case, the program of the assembly time would be unrelated to the class time. After the assembly time, students would proceed to their closely graded classes.

SIZE OF DEPARTMENTS

It is important to remember that 12 pupils are the minimum number needed to form a department, although plans may be initiated to form the department even before this number is reached in Sunday school attendance, if facilities and leadership are available. When any one department begins to reach a steady attendance of 30 pupils, it is again time to divide and form two departments instead of one. Once attendance is nearing 60, it is time to create three departments out of the previous two. In other words, departments are created on the basis of every 30 pupils (after the first department based upon 12 pupils has been created).

These departments may be divided according to the following plans. Simply making an equal numerical division of the children is the easiest way to form a new department grouping. Some may prefer to divide the children according to birthdate. For example, all those children born from January through June of a given year may form the first department group, while those born from July through December may form the second group. This plan is geared for use at the promotion period when such a new and broad formulation of department and class groupings is anticipated.

At this point it is important to determine the organizational status of your children's division on the basis of the recommended department and class sizes. Complete the following questions after securing the necessary information.

I. Number of children in attendance
   First graders (six years) _____
   Second graders (seven) _____
   Third graders (eight) _____
   Fourth graders (nine) _____
   Fifth graders (ten) _____
   Sixth graders (eleven) _____

II. Grades of children and department size
   1. Are there any grade levels where there are more than 30 children attending? _____
      Which ones? _____
   2. Are there any grade levels where there are less than 12 children attending? _____
      Which ones? _____
      How should these grade levels be grouped into departments and/or classes? _____
   3. Are there any immediate prospects available for the children's division? _____
      What are their grades? _____
      How will these additional numbers affect your planning for new departments and/or classes?
      _____

III. Available space
   1. How many department rooms are now being used for the children's division? _____
   2. Could other rooms be made available? _____ Which ones? _____
   3. Are these rooms large enough to accommodate 30 children? _____

IV. Number of departments needed
   1. How many children's departments do you now have? _____
   2. On the basis of a maximum of 30 children attending a department, how many departments should you have? _____
   3. What are the grade levels of these needed departments? _____
   4. How many departments do your room facilities allow you to have? _____

V. Available leadership
   1. How many department superintendents do you now have? _____
   2. How many additional superintendents do you need? _____
   3. On the basis that every five to eight children need to be organized into a class and need a teacher, how many teachers should you have? _____
   4. How many teachers do you now have? _____
   5. How many additional teachers do you need? _____
   6. Is the church able to provide adequate leadership for these departments and classes? _____

The organizational needs of your children's division should now be clear. Don't be discouraged if you find your children's division varying considerably from the recommended department and class group sizes. Join the club!

Many churches will find that their departments and classes are too large. This fact should signal church leadership to take immediate steps in planning that will eventually rectify the problem.

Be sure you are a vital part of the solution, not the

problem! Begin by making the organizational needs of your children's division a definite matter of prayer. Remember that God is more concerned about the effectiveness of your teaching ministry than you are. Providing appropriately organized groups that result in improved Christian education is within God's plan and purpose for the church. Do everything that you can to see that your church's children's division is organized to facilitate the teaching and learning of God's Word.

FOOTNOTES

CHAPTER 4

1 · Exodus 18:23, *King James* Version.
2 · Herman Harrell Horne, *Jesus—The Master Teacher* (New York: Association Press, 1922), pp. 140-141.
3 · Ray Rozell, *Talks on Sunday School Teaching* (Grand Rapids: Zondervan Publishing House, 1956), p. 23.

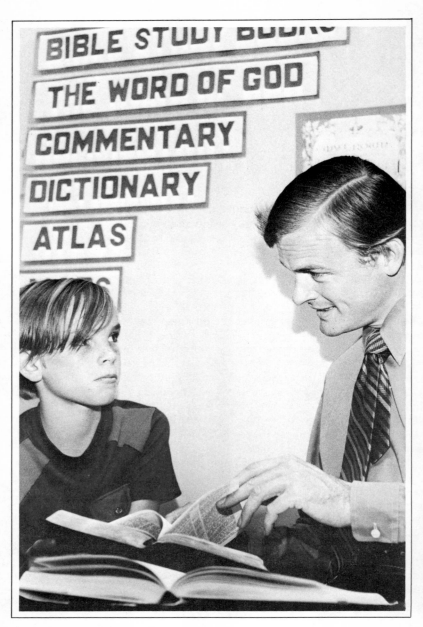

BIBLE STUDY BOOKS
THE WORD OF GOD
COMMENTARY
DICTIONARY
ATLAS

CHAPTER FIVE

ESSENTIAL LEADERSHIP ROLES

Moving Jehovah's Tabernacle could easily have been an experience of total bedlam, but divine strategy prevented any confusion. God directed Moses and his able spokesman, Aaron, to "assign duties to each man by name."[1] There were three divisions of the Levites who were responsible for the Tabernacle, and within these divisions were clans in which each man had specifically assigned duties. This was a remarkable plan when you consider the large number of males! God knew how to get the job done well!

Fortunately, your Sunday school's children's division will not need such an elaborate plan of leadership placement and division of responsibility. What little delegation of responsibility is suggested, however, will happily bring about the same end—a smoothly operating department with a considerable amount of productivity.

From its inception, the Sunday school movement has been spearheaded by lay people who have had the spiritual sensitivity and the creative genius that resulted in this systematic Bible teaching program. For some reason professionals in the work of the church failed to respond to the acute spiritual needs of the people around them.

Times have changed a little. Although the great bulk of Sunday school leadership is still drawn from the ranks of lay people, most ministers have sensed the importance of their role in the church's teaching ministry and have sought to recover it. As a result, Sunday schools have become a vital part of the average church's program, and ministers have taken definite steps to improve and enlarge them.

On the other hand, no Sunday school will rise above the quality of those church people who function at the grass roots levels of its leadership. It is these men and women who are doing the teaching and directing so essential to a Christian education program. The future of the Sunday school is still very much in their hands.

LEADERSHIP GIFTS

The Scriptures record for us the spiritual gifts necessary for the work of the church (Romans 12, 1 Corinthians 12, Ephesians 4). Every Christian has at least one spiritual gift which God has sovereignly bestowed upon him (1 Corinthians 12:7, 11). A Christian must seek to discover his spiritual gift and exercise and develop it (2 Timothy 1:6).

Of particular spiritual significance to us is the gift of teaching. A Christian who has this gift will find that the Holy Spirit actually supplies the guidance, illumination and insight so crucial to his success in the teaching ministry. Naturally, he must seek to be under the full employment of the Holy Spirit that this gift may be used to its fullest potential (Colossians 1:29, Ephesians 5:18).

Educational principles and methods are used by the gifted teacher as appropriate ways through which he can help change the spiritual lives of his pupils. After all, God devised the laws and principles of teaching and learning; He made pupils to learn according to certain developmental patterns and principles, and teachers must follow them.[2] As the teacher teaches God's Word, he is used by the Holy Spirit who applies and personalizes the Word to the pupils' lives.

The Christian who has the gift of teaching will see evidence of his gift in the response and spiritual growth of those he teaches. As he depends upon the Holy Spirit to guide and direct his teaching, the results will be effective and powerful.

The spiritually gifted teacher will grow in his realization that Christian education is much more than a human enterprise. It is a divine work in which the Holy Spirit gives both teacher and student the power to understand the truth. Christians gifted in teaching and empowered by the Holy Spirit are essential in carrying out the Sunday school's purpose in the local church.

There are other spiritual gifts that certainly have relevance to the children's Sunday school ministry. The "gift of helps" refers to those who in any way render assistance in the church, ranging from temporal affairs to directly aiding an official church leader.[3] Many people in your church have this gift and may exercise it in the children's Sunday school ministry by helping to provide and serve refreshments at a social activity, maintaining a teaching picture file, improving the room environment, or by transporting children to and from Sunday school. Some individuals will find a meaningful outlet for this gift by serving as a secretary in a children's department.

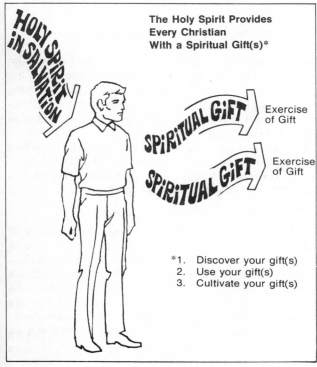

The Holy Spirit Provides Every Christian With a Spiritual Gift(s)*

Exercise of Gift

Exercise of Gift

*1. Discover your gift(s)
2. Use your gift(s)
3. Cultivate your gift(s)

Another important spiritual gift is the "gift of governments." This word was historically applied to the government or steering of a ship. Apparently those who possessed this gift were especially skilled in doing business, in presiding over group deliberations, and in directing the affairs of the church.[4] It appears that our departmental superintendents and children's division coordinators will be those individuals gifted with this skill as well as with the teaching gift.

Not all Christian teachers function well as department superintendents, since they might work best with a small group and more restricted areas of concentration. On the other hand, many individuals will possess all the gifts discussed and will function well in either the teaching or superintending role. In any event, it is of utmost importance that we seek to place Christians in the roles for which God has gifted them.

TEACHERS WHO FACILITATE LEARNING

When, as either a department superintendent or teacher, you are aware that God has bestowed upon you the teaching gift, a basic foundation for a fruitful teaching ministry is present. It is now your responsibility to cultivate this gift in every way possible so that you will have increasing skill in this role.

In one study it was found that teachers who have had remarkable success in teaching have five things in common.[5] These five factors have particular relevance to teachers of children in Sunday school.

A CLEAR VISION OF THE RESULTS INTENDED

A good teacher is not confused about the purpose of his methods or activities and their relationship to reaching the objectives he desires for his pupils. He understands how his students learn best and employs methods which facilitate this process. Furthermore, he is aware of the basic needs and learning potentials of the age group he teaches and seeks to guide his pupils in need-fulfilling learning experiences. The teacher who is sure of the teaching means and learning ends in Christian education will be a happy teacher.

The teacher who sees his main objective in his first grade class as in-depth Scripture memorization may be disappointed if the children fail to memorize large sections of verses immediately. In this case the teacher has a goal but the pupils' readiness to experience the goal is in doubt. The teacher's aims and objectives must be consistent with the age of his pupils, their home background and intellectual and emotional readiness.

A FERTILE IMAGINATION USED TO CREATE INTEREST

Variety is the spice of good teaching! To excite the interest and attention of pupils, the teacher must use a variety of approaches and methods. Pupils have a tendency to neglect the familiar, so think of unusual but relevant ways to present the truths in God's Word.

Too frequently our teaching procedures have been sterile due to the fact that we have functioned for months without any new ideas. In our teaching role we have about us a cocoon of security through which new ideas cannot penetrate. What is needed? We must stretch our minds and imaginative powers—depart from routine thinking—and allow creative teaching ideas to emerge. You will be greatly helped in this activity by reading about the general characteristics of the age of children you teach and by spending informal times playing and talking with them.

Getting creative teaching ideas is further fostered when you view the Bible lessons from the standpoint of your pupils with their varying interests, experiences and backgrounds. Approaching God's Word through our pupils' eyes should elicit some creative thoughts and ways which will make learning in Sunday school an interesting and enjoyable experience.

A SENSE OF SECURITY IN TEACHING

The person insecure about his personal involvement in teaching will frequently falter in this role. Insecurity distracts the teacher from his central task—that of structuring a life-related learning situation in which the pupil is guided into a study of God's Word that produces the maximum learning.

The teacher secure in his position has the following characteristics:

1 He knows that God has led him into teaching and he has accepted the challenges of such a position.

2 He trusts that God through the Holy Spirit is using him in this role.

3 He feels "at home" in this role, in spite of the failures and disappointments which he may experience along the way.

4 He keeps himself focused upon specific teaching goals and objectives for his pupils and uses the most suitable methods to accomplish these spiritual ends.

COMPLETE CONFIDENCE IN WHAT IS BEING TAUGHT

How important it is that leaders and teachers in the children's division have complete trust in God, depending on His word as truth. Furthermore, it is of almost equal importance that the teachers have confidence in the curriculum being used to lead the children into a solidly biblical and life-related study of the Bible.

One of the largest denominations in the United States was made aware of the importance of this point when in 1967 it had to report the loss of over 90,000 pupils in its Sunday schools over a six-year period. The denomination's educational director explained that this decline in enrollment was due to the fact that there was a growing feeling among both the teachers and pupils that the church really didn't have any genuinely "good news" to teach. What a tragedy! When there is little or no confidence in the message of the Bible and in the church's mission, we are doomed to failure.

Sometimes teachers have lost confidence in what the Sunday school teaches due to its use of teaching procedures and methods that are different and with which they are inexperienced. In such cases the teachers involved must see that the biblical message being taught is the same and that only the methods have been changed and updated for more effective teaching and learning. Such adjustments in our teaching plans are necessary if the Sunday school is going to minister to the needs of today's children. Therefore, a confidence in both the message and methods of the Sunday school is needed. A thorough teacher training program is vital in instilling this confidence.

AN UNDERSTANDING OF THE RELATIONSHIP
OF WHAT IS TAUGHT TO WHAT IS BEING LIVED

Very often there is a large gap between what our pupils know of the Bible and how they are living on the basis of this knowledge. You will remember that the Great Commission directed the disciples to teach all nations to *observe,* or practice, all of Christ's commandments. So successful were these men at this task that they were known as those who had "turned the world upside down."[6]

Yet the disciples didn't teach anything they themselves did not believe in and thoroughly live. Paul wrote that the gospel didn't come to the people at Thessalonica in mere words only, but in a powerful personalized form; God's Word was incarnate in the life of the apostle and in those who assisted him. As a result, new believers became followers of these disciples and at the same time of the Lord, setting an example for all the Christians in Macedonia and Achaia (1 Thessalonians 1:5-7).

What does this historical account mean to the Sunday school teacher? When the teacher is teaching from the center of his living experience with Jesus Christ, he is a tremendously potent tool for God! Your pupils will learn more from your life than they will from your words. We know that children identify with and imitate their adult models. Be sure that you as a teacher are an adequate spiritual model. Then expose your life to your pupils through activities in and out of the Sunday school.

Furthermore, remember that you have not truly taught, in its deepest definition, until your pupils observe or practice the truths you are teaching. "Learning in Christian education is more than the mere acquisition of ideas," stated Henrietta Mears. "It is the integration of ideas into the personality." Understanding the relationship of what is taught to what is being lived is vital to both the teacher and his pupils.

LEADERSHIP ROLES AND DUTIES

We have already referred to the four possible leadership roles in the children's division of the Sunday school. The duties of the division coordinator, department superintendent, teacher and secretary will be outlined here.

CHILDREN'S DIVISION COORDINATOR

Churches which have four or more children's departments should enlist a children's division coordinator. This person is an experienced teacher and leader who supervises and directs the work of the entire children's division of the Sunday school, grades one through six.

If the children's division has more than eight to ten departments, an additional division coordinator is needed, since good control and administration of more than this number of departments by one coordinator is extremely difficult. In such cases the division of the work will be made on the basis of younger children (grades one through three) and older children (grades four through six), with a division coordinator assigned to each area.

Only a few churches will need to be concerned about this leadership role, since most Sunday schools are adequately served by two or three children's departments and do not need a children's division coordinator. The specific duties of the children's division coordinator are:

1 Working within the framework of the church policy in discovering, recommending and enlisting personnel for the entire children's division of the Sunday school.

2 Guiding department superintendents in directing their teachers and secretaries in effective Sunday school ministry.

3 Functioning as the primary channel of communication between the Sunday school administration and the children's department superintendents.

4 Representing the children's division at the monthly Sunday school council meeting.

5 Evaluating the space and equipment in the children's division and recommending needs to the general superintendent and Sunday school council.

6 Developing and maintaining children's departments and classes of the proper size and teacher-pupil
ratio by creating new departments and classes as growth
occurs.

7 Leading department superintendents in a program
of outreach to the unenlisted children in the community.

8 Meeting monthly with the department superintendents for evaluation and planning.

9 Providing opportunities of training for prospective
and present teachers and officers.

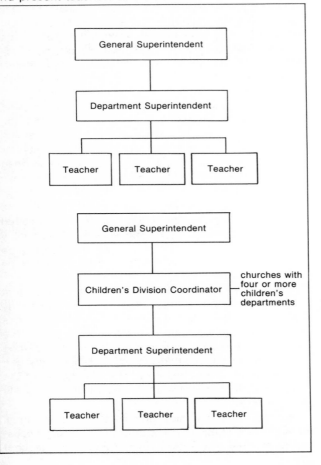

DEPARTMENT SUPERINTENDENT

A children's department superintendent carries both supervisory and teaching responsibilities. Chapter 3 pointed out the role this individual plays in the development of a unit of study. He leads his teachers in planning before each unit, including the assigning of a Bible learning activity to each teacher. The superintendent serves as a "teacher's teacher," guiding those under him in their teaching ministries. Furthermore, he introduces the unit study to the pupils on the first Sunday of the unit and guides the children in choosing a Bible learning activity. He leads the entire department in worship and in music expression. When necessary, the superintendent may serve as a substitute teacher. Children who miss the first Sunday of the unit are personally guided by the superintendent in the selection of a Bible learning activity.

He further serves as a timekeeper for the department, giving adequate notice (usually five minutes) for the ending of the class period and of the Bible learning activity period in the basic and alternate schedules. Sometimes the superintendent may merely nod his head to the teachers or flick the lights on and off as a five minute warning.

During the unit he evaluates the progress of the Bible learning activities and determines if more time is needed for their completion. If so, he may shorten his assembly period time. If the Sunday school session is to be used to its maximum potential, the time available must be carefully guarded by the superintendent.

Of utmost importance is the conclusion of the unit of study on the last Sunday. The superintendent may guide the pupils in sharing their Bible learning activities or in some other way help to evaluate the effect of the unit. He further seeks to guide the children in their explanation of the relationship of the Bible study unit to their attitudes and behavior. The conclusion of the unit will be a key time for pupils to respond in appropriate decision making.

Once the unit is completed, the teachers will meet for evaluation of this study and for the planning necessary for the new unit. This is an important time of teacher development and builds the department personnel into a strong teaching team. Listed below are the department superintendent's general duties:

1   Working within the framework of the church policy in discovering, recommending and enlisting personnel for the Sunday school department.

2   Helping department teachers and officers to fulfill their assignments.

3   Functioning as the channel of communication between the general Sunday school superintendent or children's division coordinator and teachers and secretary.

4   Representing the department at the monthly Sunday school council meeting. (This task may be done by the division coordinator.)

5   Evaluating the space and equipment and recommending needs to the general superintendent or coordinator.

6   Building the proper ratio of teacher to students by creating needed classes as growth occurs.

7   Leading in a program of outreach in order to find those who are not enlisted in Sunday school.

8   Seeking to develop and maintain a plan in which the teachers effectively enlist the cooperation of the parents of their pupils in deepening the impact of the Sunday school's education ministry.

TEACHER

The teacher is of paramount importance, since he is the means of personalizing God's Word to the lives of individual pupils.

You will recall from chapter 3 that the teacher is responsible for two blocks of time in the Sunday session. He teaches the Bible lesson to his permanent class group and leads one of the temporary Bible learning activity groups.

It is important that every teacher have a class group which he can teach and cultivate spiritually. The Bible story can be taught more effectively in the small class group due in part to the potentially greater personal interaction between teacher and pupils. The small class group will also tend to sustain pupil attention and interest in the Bible story.

Furthermore, when the teacher teaches the Bible story to his class group, he has the Bible background essential to making the Bible learning activity period a more effective time of teaching Bible content and its relationship to life. When the department superintendent or a master department teacher teaches the lesson, the teachers are not forced to study it thoroughly. Thus they may lack information essential to the use of these activities as a tool of learning. We can't expect our pupils to do something that the teacher has not done himself. There is a spiritual and emotional value to this procedure too, since teachers who teach the Bible story are usually more spiritually excited through this experience, and this enthusiasm is contagious!

It is recommended that each permanent class grouping of pupils in at least the fifth and sixth grades be divided on the basis of sex, with a man teacher for the boys and a woman for the girls. Some churches prefer to follow this principle for all children's classes regardless of the grade. It is true that men and women teachers are needed in each children's department, but it is not essential that the first three or four grades of classes be divided solely on the basis of sex, with a corresponding teacher.

There will be ample opportunity for children of both sexes to be together in the assembly group and especially in the small temporary groups where the Bible learning activities are used.

Each teacher should provide the opportunity for his pupils to receive Christ as their personal Saviour and Lord. In chapter 1 some basic guidelines are given to the teacher for his use in leading children to a personal faith in Christ. Follow them! The opportunity to speak personally to your pupils regarding this decision will frequently develop out of the class lesson period as you unfold the Bible story.

If a pupil wishes to accept Christ, deal with him personally, perhaps when the rest of your class has gone on to the large assembly group. Your department superintendent will understand the nature of your delay and will be able to cover for you in your brief absence. Nothing is quite as exciting as guiding a child into a meaningful discovery of Jesus Christ as personal Saviour!

The following list of duties further defines the teacher's important role:

1 Guiding your permanent class group in a life-related study of God's Word.

2 Guiding your temporary Bible learning activities groups in active and meaningful research and expression of assigned study projects.

3 Cultivating the friendship and interests of assigned pupils and their families.

4 Leading your pupils into a progressive understanding of spiritual awareness and experience with Jesus Christ and His church.

5 Assisting the department superintendent in regular evaluation and planning at monthly department meetings.

6 Cooperating with the department superintendent and other teachers in discovering and reaching prospects and their families.

7 Engaging in class and individual study opportunities that will improve your effectiveness.

SECRETARY

If a children's department has only 12 to 18 children in attendance, a secretary is not essential. The department superintendent may care for the record keeping while the teachers are guiding their classes in a study of the Bible story at the first part of the Sunday school session.

Even in the smallest of departments, however, a secretary will play a useful role. Although his major responsibilities are directly tied to maintaining the department record system, other functions are frequently assumed by a competent secretary. He may step in for a teacher who has been detained in his arrival to class. He should also take a keen interest in the appearance of the room and seek to improve it.

Generally he will be the first person that the pupils see upon their arrival, and his friendly greeting may help to set the stage for a happy learning experience.

Very often there will be other opportunities through which he can personally minister in brief but meaningful ways to individual pupils. An acquaintance with the records will enable him to know each child by name and to encourage them in their Bible study and regular attendance of Sunday school sessions.

Here is a list of the secretary's duties:

1 Working in cooperation with the general Sunday school secretary and the department superintendent with regard to the records system.

2 Maintaining the department records system with accuracy.

3 Warmly greeting and welcoming pupils from his table near the entrance to the room.

4 Receiving, recording, reporting and submitting departmental offerings to the general Sunday school secretary.

5 Studying and analyzing the records, reporting any information helpful to improving the department ministry to its pupils.

6 Assisting in preparing absentee follow-up information and/or materials for the teachers.

7 Attending the monthly department officers planning meeting.

The number of leaders that will be necessary to staff your children's Sunday school division will depend upon the number of children included in grades one through six. The number of department superintendents will depend upon the number of departments you are able to have on the basis of available space and the number of children. The number of teachers will be closely linked to the number of class groups you are able to form, preferably no less than one for every five to eight pupils.

RATING YOUR LEADERSHIP QUALITY IN THE TEACHING MINISTRY

Regardless of your role in the Sunday school's teaching ministry, a deep commitment to your duties is vital. The Scriptures clearly state that a steward should be found faithful (1 Corinthians 4:2). Fidelity or reliability is the crucial test of quality Christian leadership. Are you a faithful steward or leader in the use and cultivation of your spiritual gifts in the service of Christ and His church?

Rating yourself on the basis of the following statements will help you evaluate your present service in the children's division of the Sunday school, especially if you are directly tied into the teaching role as a department superintendent or teacher.

On the number scale below, circle the number that you feel best represents your present level of achievement. Five indicates the highest level; zero indicates that the particular statement in question does not relate to your area of service. Following this exercise, place a check in the box next to the statements where you plan improvements in the coming year.

PERSONAL LIFE

☐ I live a life that is consistent with Christian teaching.　　0 1 2 3 4 5

☐ I engage in daily prayer, realizing the importance of it in my own spiritual growth.　　0 1 2 3 4 5

☐ I devote time each day to personal Bible study and meditation.　　0 1 2 3 4 5

☐ I am regular in church attendance and participate in activities designed for my spiritual growth.　　0 1 2 3 4 5

☐ I systematically support the financial program of my church, following scriptural admonitions regarding this phase of Christian stewardship.　　0 1 2 3 4 5

☐ I regularly share my Christian faith with those who do not know Christ.　　0 1 2 3 4 5

☐ I am motivated to be a part of the children's Sunday school ministry because Christ is my life, and His desire is to reach and teach others through me.　　0 1 2 3 4 5

☐ I constantly observe children in order to gain a better understanding of them and to improve my ministry with them.　　0 1 2 3 4 5

TEACHING ACTIVITY

☐ I establish a meaningful relationship with each pupil through various means of contact.　　0 1 2 3 4 5

☐ I devote the necessary amount of time each week in preparation for the lesson and related Bible learning activities.　　0 1 2 3 4 5

☐ I attend the departmental planning meetings and/or workers' conferences.　　0 1 2 3 4 5

☐ I take advantage of the opportunities for teacher training and further Bible study.　　0 1 2 3 4 5

☐ I am regular and punctual in my place of responsibility.　　0 1 2 3 4 5

☐ I prayerfully guide my pupils into spiritual experiences appropriate to their present stage of intellectual, emotional and spiritual development, conscious that each such experience will eventually contribute to conversion and/or Christian growth.　　0 1 2 3 4 5

☐ I express a willingness to change when more effective methods of teaching children are discovered.　　0 1 2 3 4 5

☐ I work cooperatively with the other teachers and departmental officers, realizing the benefits that come through such a team relationship in Christian education.　　0 1 2 3 4 5

☐ I assist in the outreach efforts of the department as it seeks to minister to prospective pupils.　　0 1 2 3 4 5

☐ I depend on the Holy Spirit to use God's Word to accomplish His purpose.　　0 1 2 3 4 5

☐ I believe that the Word of God is more important than my word.　　0 1 2 3 4 5

HOME INVOLVEMENT

☐ I pray regularly for my pupils and for the homes they represent.　　0 1 2 3 4 5

☐ I encourage Christian education in the homes of my pupils through counsel with their parents.　　0 1 2 3 4 5

☐ I seek to offer a spiritual ministry to each family. 0 1 2 3 4 5

☐ I contact absentee pupils and seek to determine the reason for their absence. 0 1 2 3 4 5

☐ I make regular visits to the pupils' homes, interpreting the teaching content and suggesting ways in which the parents may augment the Sunday school's ministry. 0 1 2 3 4 5

☐ I attempt to reach my pupils' families if they are not yet Christians and/or attending church. 0 1 2 3 4 5

FOOTNOTES

CHAPTER 5

1 · Numbers 4:32, *The Living Bible* (Wheaton: Tyndale House, Publishers, 1971). Used by permission.
2 · Roy Zuck, *The Holy Spirit in Your Teaching* (Wheaton: Scripture Press Publications, 1963), p. 76.
3 · Albert Barnes, *Barnes' Notes on the New Testament* (Grand Rapids: Kregel Publications, 1962), p. 768.
4 · Barnes, *Barnes' Notes on the New Testament*, p. 768.
5 · B. F. Jackson, Jr., ed., *Communication: Learning for Churchmen, Vol. 1* (Nashville: Abingdon Press, 1968), pp. 180-182.
6 · Acts 17:6, *King James Version.*

CHAPTER SIX

FACILITIES TEACH TOO

The most effective environment for spiritual growth and learning is the everyday happenings of living. God directed Moses to command parents to teach the law to their children within the experiences of this natural life context. It was within this practical environment that God's truth took on real meaning and relevance to Jewish offspring as they worked and played in their daily environment.

Jesus in His teaching ministry used this broad, natural environment too. His teaching was based on the immediate occasion in which He found, or divinely placed, Himself. He taught in a spontaneous fashion at all hours, under varying circumstances and in all places.

Christ always used the environment to His advantage in teaching. Fishing led to fishing for men. A well led to a revelation of "living water." A mountain or a boat became a speaker platform. A sea storm provided an opportunity to deepen belief.

Today's teacher needs to recognize the teaching opportunities inherent in the normal life-environment and the resulting implications for his role. As previously mentioned, parents are the main educators of their children. From time to time they need our assistance and suggestions in converting everyday circumstances and surroundings into positive learning experiences. The sensitive teacher should be alert to opportunities to see that Christian teaching is applied to situations which arise spontaneously in and out of the classroom.

Furthermore, the classroom environment should take

on a less formal and traditional feeling and appearance. Christ taught in real-life surroundings and situations. He took the real, vital life situation at hand and turned it into a relevant lesson. We need to bring into our classrooms some of the warmth and informality of a home and the freedom of the outdoors.

Have you ever wondered about the vast amount of learning which takes place during a child's preschool years at home? Learning during this period is efficient and effortless compared to much of the child's formal schooling in later years. Why? Out of natural curiosity and need, the child is constantly interacting with people and immediate surroundings, discovering for himself information and concepts which are relevant to him at a particular time.

Too often we miss the opportunity of meaningful learning by putting this eager learner into a formal classroom, placing him into a passive role and then wondering that he is so hard to teach. Obviously, we should be analyzing the learning experiences we are trying to provide for our pupils. Are they guided to explore and discover Bible teachings for their lives? Are they using all of their five senses? Is mutual respect fostered and involvement encouraged—both mental and physical? Is there as much pupil expression as there is teacher impression?

By choice, most children spend a lot of time outdoors where they can move and play more freely. A feeling of outdoor freedom can be fostered when pupils are given the opportunity to move about in the classroom (primarily during activity time) and to choose how they will study the Scripture being taught. Freedom to probe, ask questions, use their imaginations and share ideas and solutions is fostered in a more informal outdoorslike environment. In this way learning is more meaningful.

ROOM SHAPE AND ENVIRONMENT

Up to this point our discussion has centered mainly on the intangible or nonmaterial environment for learning. Some educators have described the material or physical room environment as the "third partner" in classroom education (the teacher and pupil being the first two).

Some Sunday school personnel have underestimated the importance of this part of the learning environment, but most children's teachers are sensitive to it. The growing feeling among alert teachers of children, however, is that our children need the best possible learning environment. Your room is that silent partner which can aid or hinder pupil behavior, shape or crush curriculum and teaching methods, encourage or stifle the attainment of goals and results.

There has always been considerable diversity in Sunday school room design for children. Many churches constructed the traditional assembly room with small classrooms surrounding it (Diagram 1). First through sixth grade teaching programs seemed to adapt themselves well to this arrangement, providing for class group instruction as well as large group worship and other assembly activities.

Diagram 1

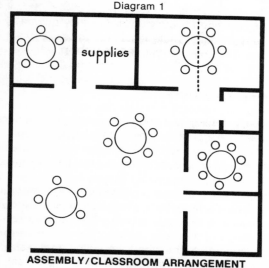

ASSEMBLY/CLASSROOM ARRANGEMENT

Other churches have carried on effective teaching programs in open rooms (those having no small classrooms adjoining the assembly room). (See Diagram 2.) In this situation class groups have met around tables in various corners of the room. Absence of sight and sound barriers has not proven to be a problem; children have been conditioned to learning in an open room in public school. Individual pupil needs are still met, while group spirit has been fostered in the entire department.

Diagram 2

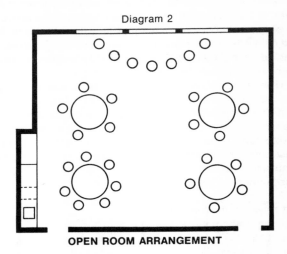

OPEN ROOM ARRANGEMENT

PLANNING GUIDELINES

Are you planning to remodel or build new children's facilities? Several factors need to be considered.

First, the expense of construction is soaring. The more walls necessary to a department, the greater the cost will be.

Second, more churches are realizing the importance of building rooms which will function adequately for other activities and age groups. Often the design and construction of a purely "children's department room" has eliminated other usage. Depending on the size and quality of a church's physical plant and program, this may or may not be an important factor.

Third, the trend in Christian education for the seventies is definitely toward a more flexible teaching procedure, providing for a broader use of teaching involvement methods and greater teacher cooperation. Teaching children in this way may be easier in an open room environment in which the department superintendent can easily direct, observe, evaluate and assist in small and large groups. Closed classroom doors have too frequently locked out the superintendent from this, his primary role.

Fourth, disciplinary problems tend to be fewer in an open room structure. Children are influenced by observing their peers actively engaged in meaningful learning experiences. They tend to imitate the actions of one another and work more enthusiastically because everyone else is working.

Fifth, increased flexibility in grouping pupils results from use of the open room. For instance, two class groups may desire to see the same filmstrip and can easily move their chairs together without disturbing the other class groups.

Sixth, the shift from class groups to large groups and then to activity groups is handled with less wasted time and physical movement.

Seventh, teaching-learning resources are easily available to all teachers and pupils in the open room. Art materials need not be duplicated for each class but can be quickly and easily shared.

OPENING A CLOSED ROOM

Earlier we discussed how effectively Christ taught in all types of environments. Nevertheless, many teachers are limited by a small room atmosphere and a short instruction period. They should still be very careful to create a good learning environment. Whether in an open room or in a classroom/assembly room arrangement, this environment does not just happen—the teacher "builds" or "molds" it.

Some of the advantages of an open room environment can be created in classroom/assembly room situations. Here are some suggestions:

1　Remove the doors from the small classrooms or allow them to stand open during session.

2　Place at least one of your classes and/or activity groups in the assembly area.

3   Use one of your classrooms as a resource or supply center.

4   Blend together all of the rooms through complementary colors and equipment.

5   Encourage the department superintendents to move about the classrooms, observing the learning activity and being alert to needs to which they can respond.

STANDARDS FOR SPACE

There are room space standards by which each children's department should be measured if good teaching is to be achieved. We need to know these standards and consider our own facilities in relation to them.

There has been considerable diversity in the size of children's rooms and thus diversity in the number of pupils contained in them. A few churches have provided huge rooms where 50 to 100 pupils have been taught. More frequently, however, churches have provided rooms that are far too small and have crowded too many pupils into them. Almost always the end result of both these extremes is poor Bible teaching, not to mention tired-out, frustrated teachers and restless pupils. For these reasons here are some guidlines that will aid in any remodeling or new construction of children's rooms.

FLOOR SPACE

Twenty-five to 30 square feet of floor space per person should be provided in each children's department. As pointed out earlier, the recommended maximum attendance in each department is 30.

Your educational planners may feel that you are providing too much space in a children's room, but this is by no means true. Let's be sure that our students are not placed like a carpet—wall-to-wall—but given enough room to participate in creative learning of God's truth.

GROWTH SPACE

The right-sized room, however, may also be filled to the point of growth stagnation. When your department attendance begins to exceed 30, plans should be made for the addition of another department.

Studies in church growth have shown that when a group has grown to occupy 75 percent of its available space, it begins to stagnate as a result of what is called growth strangulation. The room strangles further growth (a psychological-physical phenomenon). Since we are working toward the growth of our Sunday schools, our children's departments should be kept at a size where the maximum teaching can be carried out and further growth stimulated.

ROOM LOCATION

Under most circumstances it is recommended that children's rooms be located on a first or second floor level and near an exit opening onto a main corridor. Children's rooms should be grouped together with attractive landscaping that can be seen by the children through low windows.

FURTHER CONSIDERATIONS

Other matters to consider are restrooms, drinking fountains and sinks. It is most desirable to place restrooms near all children's rooms. Younger children will benefit from a restroom adjoining their department. Some churches have provided children's lavatories between every two department rooms. Sinks and drinking facilities are recommended for all children's rooms; a combination unit is popular in public schools. Having water nearby will be a great asset as more creative methods of instruction are used (i.e., art and construction activities).

Generally, churches have provided adequate wall space for bulletin boards and chalkboards. Sometimes, however, these items have not been logically placed at the proper height or at centers of attention that are related to room shape and seating arrangement. (Check for proper heights on equipment lists at the end of this chapter.)

Walls themselves need to be soundproof and painted in cheerful colors. Recent research released by the American Medical Association disclosed that children's grades rose noticeably when their study rooms were decorated in attractive yellow. Bright colors are stimulating and exciting and are used most effectively in small areas. Pale colors, like pale yellow and white, suggest sunshine and look good on large wall areas. Dark walls can be gloomy and depressing unless accented with white, for example, and well lighted. Blues and greens create a feeling of coolness, which makes them good choices for rooms that get hot southern and western sunlight. Color can also change the apparent size of a room, hide undesirable features and emphasize desirable ones. So choose your color wisely; let it be a supportive element in the teaching-learning process.

Floors and ceilings should be complementary in color and should provide sound absorption. White acoustical ceilings are quite common in school construction.

There is a growing trend in Sunday school rooms of using carpet instead of tile or linoleum. The initial cost (material and installation) is, of course, higher, but the maintenance of carpet is less costly than that of tile and therefore less expensive in the long run. There are many pros and cons regarding the use of carpet. Its most positive contribution to a children's learning environment is the quietness and warmth it provides. And it is of definite value acoustically. For an open room environment, carpeting is ideal, but a good tile (vinyl or vinyl asbestos) will serve if necessary.

Lighting of children's rooms is an all-important factor. Lighting standards for public schools have steadily increased over the past twenty years, and architects now recommend higher wattage to provide adequate light for reading and paper and pencil activity. Remember that floor, wall and ceiling color can either reflect light or absorb it, so be sure to check your color.

MAKING THE MOST OF THE SPACE YOU HAVE

An analysis of your children's rooms on the basis of these standards should provide the necessary information to evaluate your circumstances. After you have noted the areas needing improvement, formulate a simple plan to make any necessary changes.

Unfortunately, some children's Sunday school rooms are a picture of neglect. Lighting, ventilation and color schemes are poor. Unfinished walls and floors are common, and the furniture may be an odd collection of items suitable in size only because of its height. Storage space may be scarce and cluttered with odds and ends. Such shabbiness can be easily remedied through the efforts of the department workers and other willing volunteers. If teachers and parents are really interested in better teaching, they should take a long, hard look at the classroom environment and then act.

The typical children's teacher or leader will be limited in effecting immediate, major physical improvements such as the construction of new or additional children's rooms or the installation of lavatories.

Considerable progress can be made, however, in areas that can tangibly improve the learning environment. Are your rooms clean and cheerfully painted? Do you have a bulletin board and chalkboard in your room and are they placed at pupil eye level? Can light bulb wattage be increased for a somewhat dark room? Is there a room which could be converted into another children's room to aid in growth? Is there a carpenter in the church who could volunteer to lower and/or enlarge your rooms' windows? Could the carpenter also build needed equipment or alter your chairs to conform to the children's height? Could the church trustees budget new floor covering (carpet or vinyl asbestos) for your room with church members putting it down? Such plans, relatively low in cost, can improve a learning environment and make your teaching more effective.

EQUIPPING FOR LEARNING

A learning environment is incomplete without necessary equipment which aids both the teacher and the pupil. Earlier we pointed out the necessity for bulletin boards and chalkboards, but generally these are considered standard items which most rooms have. The following lists with specifications for first through sixth grades discuss the various pieces of equipment necessary for an effective learning environment.

CHAIRS

The nonfolding type of chair is recommended. Many churches have found the tubular, steel-frame chair with a plastic seat and back, which is stackable, to be quite adequate and durable.

Specifications for grades 1 to 3: The height should be 12 to 14 inches for first and second graders and 14 to 15 inches high for third graders.

Grades 4 to 6: The height should be 14 to 15 inches for fourth and fifth graders and 16 inches for sixth graders.

TABLES

Rectangular tables (Diagram 3) are recommended. The kidney-shaped and trapezoidal tables are also widely used.

The rectangular and trapezoidal tables are the most versatile; they may be pushed squarely against the wall to free floor space for other activities or fit together to make a large square around which two small groups of children may gather.

The kidney-shaped table is popular because the teacher is close to all of the pupils, and each pupil is placed around the teacher in a half-circle. On the other hand, this table does not have the versatility of the rectangular table and, depending on the size of the class group, may place a couple of pupils behind the teacher, at his extreme left and right. Long rectangular tables take up too much space, are difficult to move and make it hard for the pupils to work together. Adjustable legs are desirable, and the table should be 10 inches above the chair seat height. A small secretarial table (approximately 24 by 30 inches) should be placed at the room's entrance.

Specifications for grades 1 to 3: The tables should be no smaller than 30 by 48 inches and no larger than 36 by 60 inches.

Grades 4 to 6: The tables should be approximately 36 by 60 inches.

Diagram 3

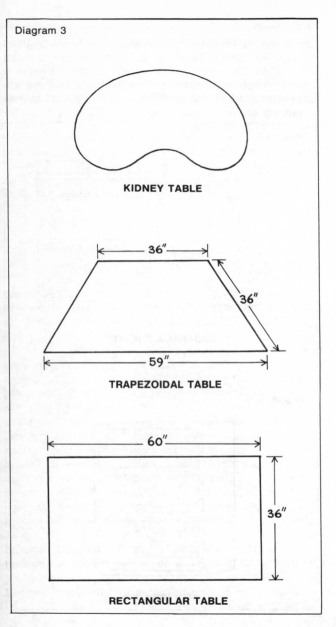

KIDNEY TABLE

36″

36″

59″

TRAPEZOIDAL TABLE

60″

36″

RECTANGULAR TABLE

BOOKRACK

Since guided reading and research activity will be used in Sunday school sessions, a bookrack with slanted shelves to display book titles or subject matter is a helpful piece of equipment. The height should be approximately 42 inches and the width about 36 inches (Diagram 4).

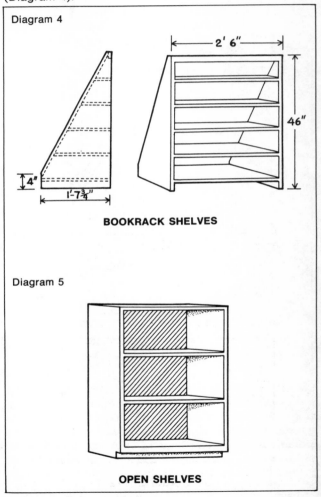

Diagram 4

BOOKRACK SHELVES

Diagram 5

OPEN SHELVES

SHELVES

An open shelf cabinet with three shelves will be helpful for displaying various objects related to the current Bible study. Supplies for learning activities or projects may also be stored on the shelves, making them easily accessible to the pupils who are using them during a unit of study (Diagram 5).

Specifications for grades 1 to 3: The shelves should be at least 12 inches apart and 12 inches deep with a height of 39 to 42 inches and a length of 36 to 42 inches.

Grades 4 to 6: The shelves should be at least 12 to 14 inches apart and 12 to 14 inches deep with a height of 46 to 48 inches and a length of 42 to 48 inches.

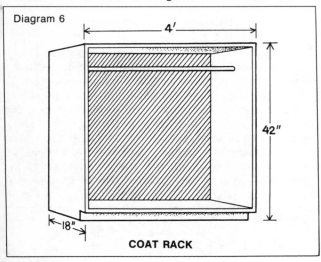

Diagram 6

4'

42"

18"

COAT RACK

COATRACK

Each room should have a coatrack or coat hooks for the children's coats. Rounded wooden pegs are excellent for hanging up the coats. If preferred, the rack may be portable (Diagram 6), or it may be built into the storage cabinet area (Diagram 7). An adult rack is not essential, but if provided, it should be at least 54 to 60 inches above the floor, while the children's rack should be about 42 inches from the floor.

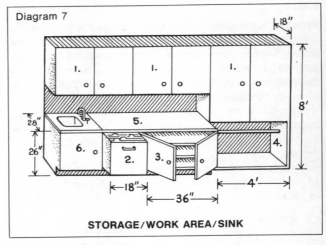

STORAGE/WORK AREA/SINK

STORAGE CABINETS

The wall-to-ceiling hung cabinet is often preferred, since it does not take up valuable floor space (Diagram 8). A room may be planned, however, to include a cabinet, sink and coatrack area which can avoid taking up undue amounts of floor space (Diagram 7). Cabinets should be 18 inches deep, allowing for room to store such items as large construction paper. Adequate space should be provided for other groups that may be using the room, possibly allowing for each group a cabinet area that may be locked separately.

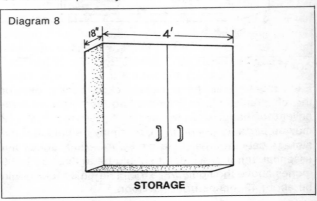

STORAGE

PIANO

Generally, the studio size piano with large casters is preferred, but very often a room is equipped with used or gift pianos. Large, upright pianos have often been painted the color of the room to call less attention to them. Many teachers have found that an Autoharp, cassette, or record player is preferable to a piano.

CHALKBOARDS

Older children and their teachers will use a chalkboard more frequently than younger age groups. An assembly room should have a board permanently installed that is about 3 by 5 feet or 4 by 6 feet in size (the larger preferred). The chalk rail may also serve as a picture rail. Small classrooms located off a large assembly room should each have a chalkboard of no larger than 3 feet by 5 feet in size.

Specifications for grades 1 to 3: All boards should be placed from 28 to 30 inches above the floor.

Grades 4 to 6: All boards should be placed 32 inches above the floor.

BULLETIN BOARDS

The most expensive boards are cork, but fiberboard is an inexpensive and satisfactory substitute. Fiberboard may be purchased at a lumberyard or building supply center and covered with burlap, other fabrics or paper. It should not be painted, as the paint will make it too hard for pins to penetrate easily. Two large bulletin boards are adequate for an assembly or open department room, sized according to the wall space available. These boards should be anywhere from 4 to 12 feet long (the larger, the better) and from 3 to 4 feet high. When small classrooms are provided, each should have a smaller bulletin board from 2½ to 3 feet high and from 3 to 4 feet long.

Specifications for grades 1 to 3: The boards should be mounted approximately 28 to 30 inches above the floor.

Grades 4 to 6: The boards should be mounted approximately 32 inches above the floor.

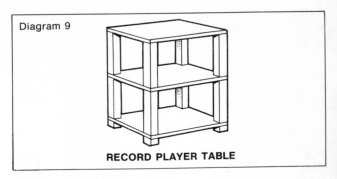

Diagram 9

RECORD PLAYER TABLE

RECORD PLAYER AND TABLE

Music is an integral part of teaching Sunday school, so a record player and a small table or cabinet to place it on will be very useful. The table (Diagram 9) should be small (approximately 16 inches by 16 inches on top). Records not in use may be stored on a shelf beneath the tabletop or in a storage cabinet. A record storage cabinet may be purchased or constructed by a cabinet-maker. The record player should have three speeds and be durable enough to allow the children to use it many times.

SOLVING EQUIPMENT PROBLEMS

The majority of churches will be unable to immediately provide all of the recommended equipment. Therefore, each leader should find adequate substitutes for those most essential items.

You may need to use rugs or mats instead of chairs or to alter the legs of old adult chairs to fit children.

Lapboards (12 by 18 inches) may serve as table substitutes. At times, children may even work comfortably on a clean floor, although it is a bit more difficult for the adult teachers! Old tables may be altered to fit the children's height, just as we suggested regarding chairs. Moreover, such tables can have a laminated plastic top glued onto them, greatly improving their appearance and durability. Benches may serve a dual purpose as both tables and chairs, but only as a last resort.

Other equipment items may be temporarily provided through ingenuity. Open shelves may serve as a bookrack. A box may be used as storage for a picture file or supplies or as a table for art supplies or books during the Sunday school session. A large sheet of cardboard or fiberboard may be leaned against a wall or hung for a bulletin board. Such suggestions are ideally adapted to mission churches which must rent facilities that are not considered educational. Much effective teaching can be accomplished in such an environment when the effort is made to improvise and thus create a good learning environment.

TEACHERS NEED TO LEARN TOO!

"How seldom the Sunday school teacher is asked for his credentials!" This statement reflected Dr. Henrietta Mears' concern for quality Christian education. She knew this goal could never be achieved if the Sunday school was "managed by a few willing but untrained enthusiasts." Her convictions on this subject are amplified in the following quotation: "A public school teacher is not questioned as to whether he will teach, but rather, can he teach. Our request in securing Sunday school teachers is invariably, 'Will you take a class?' And good-natured men and women, much against their wills, answer, 'I will keep the class going until you find someone else.' If a math teacher is absent, can you imagine the principal going out in the neighborhood, ringing doorbells and asking a housewife, 'Will you come over and take a class in mathematics because the regular teacher is sick?' Absurd! He notifies the superintendent's office of his need, and a trained person comes."[1]

Our standards for Sunday school leadership are frequently too low and reflect a deficient view of the church's educational ministry. A basic function of the church is to teach the Holy Scriptures, which are our sole guide for living the Christian faith. To do less than our best at this task is spiritual negligence. And competent Sunday school leadership is the pivotal point upon which the success of this entire ministry rests.

Here are some relevant questions regarding leadership and teacher training.

1   What is expected of Sunday school teachers?

2 How should you qualify for teaching in your Sunday school?

3 Is teacher training provided?

4 Do you consider such training optional or essential?

5 Are the teachers grounded biblically and theologically?

6 Do you understand the age group characteristics of the children you teach?

7 Is the church's childhood educational philosophy clearly understood and practiced?

8 Are monthly teachers' meetings held?

9 Do all workers feel the necessity of meeting together for evaluation, planning, study and prayer?

These questions should stimulate consideration of the crucial role teacher training plays in the spiritual vitality of the children's Sunday school ministry.

AREAS OF NEEDED TRAINING

Let us look at our Sunday school and the roles of the leadership to grasp some of the training needed to make this institution productive. There are three basic areas in which training is needed: Bible knowledge and theology, age group characteristics and psychological and educational techniques.

BIBLE KNOWLEDGE AND THEOLOGY

Adequate and appropriate knowledge of the basic doctrines is a must in the teacher's ministry. This information is the content of the Sunday school's teaching ministry. If a teacher is unclear on what the Bible teaches and communicates, his hazy understanding of a story or theological truth will cause pupil misconceptions. Paul instructed the young minister Timothy, "Take heed unto thyself, and unto the doctrine; continue in them: for in doing this thou shalt both save thyself, and them that hear thee."[2]

If Christians wait until they are thoroughly saturated in Bible truth to engage in teaching, however, God's program might be stifled. Timothy and the apostles before him had an adequate knowledge of God's revelation before they were actively teaching, but by no means did they know it all. They were constantly growing in their understanding while teaching what they knew. Timothy was urged to "study to show thyself approved unto God, a workman that needeth not to be ashamed, rightly dividing the word of truth."[3] To be an "approved" Bible student is the goal, and serving as a teacher will help you reach this goal more rapidly. As Dr. Wilbur Smith has stated, "Teaching does not provide a reason for Bible study; it creates the necessity."[4]

The church's teacher training program must be partially directed to meet the spiritual needs of the teacher. Teachers should acquire a certain mastery of the Bible and its teaching regarding God, Jesus Christ, the Holy Spirit, man, salvation, revelation, angels, the church and future events. You may not always feel the necessity for this background nor use it directly in your teaching, but it will enrich your own life and be a resource upon which you may draw in both the classroom and other teaching opportunities.

AGE-GROUP CHARACTERISTICS AND PSYCHOLOGY

A good teacher understands his pupils. Though every child is different from another, some general age group characteristics are common to each stage of childhood. Barbara Bolton, in her book, *Ways to Help Them Learn: Children*[5] has carefully identified these age group characteristics. As a prelude to successful childhood education in the church, teachers should study the portions of this book which deal with these childhood characteristics.

Knowing and understanding these childhood characteristics will help you to grasp the psychology of the age group you teach. This understanding of their mental nature and behavior will give you educational insight. You will see that for the pupils to learn best, certain methods need to be used during the Sunday school session. Christian education should be related to the developmental period or age through which your pupils are passing at a particular time if it is to be spiritually and educationally effective. Know your pupils!

EDUCATIONAL TECHNIQUES

In His teaching ministry, Jesus demonstrated the importance of educational techniques in God's plan of reaching and equipping people for abundant living. Return to chapter 2 and read again the Master Teacher's use of educational principles and techniques. Follow in His steps!

Teachers of children should study *Ways to Help Them Learn: Children* for a thorough explanation of childhood teaching techniques applicable to the Sunday school. Approaches, procedures and methods essential to the teaching-learning process are explained in detail in this companion volume.

It is at this point that many of our Sunday schools have fallen behind. Some teachers are content to stick with the methods they have always used and have not been guided toward using a variety of creative methods that may improve the teaching-learning process. Teachers have also followed rigid time schedules for Sunday school sessions when more flexibility and variety would help to stimulate pupil interest in learning.

Our teaching techniques must include gaining the cooperation of the parents of our pupils. In the Preface of this book the historical role of the Sunday school was stated. This agency is to stimulate and guide parents in their strategic roles as the prime educators of their children as well as to augment parental instruction and to provide a biblical education for children whose parents are not Christians. In the latter case, teachers should seek to win non-Christian parents to Christ, thus providing the environment which is needed for a productive Christian education. Training teachers in improved educational techniques is of paramount importance to the success of the children's division of the Sunday school.

WAYS OF TRAINING

How shall teachers be trained for a productive ministry with children? Historically, the Sunday school movement has used a variety of ways to develop teachers: teachers' helps in the curriculum, magazines, books, conventions, institutes, classes or course studies. Each of these ways is used in preparing today's Sunday school teachers.

In a 1970 survey among teachers in evangelical Sunday school a number of interesting facts came to light regarding teacher training. Among the kinds of training and help received by teachers before they began teaching were a teachers meeting or workers conference (50.3%), a teacher training course(s) (39.4%), reading a magazine(s), book(s) or booklet(s) on teaching (37%) and serving as an assistant or substitute teacher (33.1%).

Twenty-five percent of those surveyed stated that they had had a briefing session with the superintendent and/or teachers regarding teaching materials and procedures. Over 22 percent indicated that no training or help was received before they assumed their teaching positions.[6]

After assuming their teaching roles, these same teachers evaluated the kinds of training and help received and ranked teacher training courses as the most helpful (35%). Teachers meetings at church ranked second (31.8%). Although the course method of teacher training was evaluated as the most helpful, over 42 percent of those surveyed had not participated in this type of training.[7]

The kind of training most desired by teachers participating in this survey was teachers meetings (39.6%) and teacher training courses (39%). Reading magazines, books or booklets ranked third (27.6%), while visiting another Sunday school for new ideas ranked fourth (25.8%). Listening to a record and/or viewing a film or filmstrip ranked fifth (21.9%).[8]

Leaders of children's Sunday schools should provide the types of help and training that are the most effective and desirable for their personnel. Teachers meetings and training courses are essential elements in a successful training program.

Of further importance is the use of quality Christian education literature—magazines, books and booklets.

In-service training and observation activity must also play a part in a thorough training plan. Teachers, like pupils, learn best in different ways, and our training program must provide for diversity if it is to be productive.

An effective Sunday school teaching ministry among children is impossible without frequent leadership planning meetings. The type of teaching recommended in this book makes the meeting of teachers a necessity, especially on the individual department level. This teaching requires teamwork. The unit thrust needs to be carefully planned. Each teacher should know the unit teaching aims, learning readiness activities, Bible stories, memory verses and songs and the Bible learning activities. Every facet of the total teaching session should be a concern of each, since it is through the sum total of these activities that most effective teaching can be accomplished. This total view of the Sunday school session and how each part works together with the other parts is one of the chief accomplishments of frequent teachers meetings.

BENEFITS OF FREQUENT MEETINGS

But that is not all! Note the following list of educational benefits relating to frequent departmental staff meetings.

1   Curriculum materials can be previewed, then thoroughly studied, understood and put to the best and wisest use.

2   Previous sessions can be evaluated.

3   Plans can be made to correct weaknesses.

4   Plans can be made to trim the sessions of activity which does not contribute to the teaching of the Scriptures, thus conserving teaching time.

5   Needed changes in scheduling may be clarified and initiated.

6   Teaching plans for each unit of study may be detailed, including the assignment of a Bible learning activity to each teacher.

7   Supplies necessary for teaching activities may be determined and gathered for Sunday use.

8   Methods of teaching may be demonstrated and practiced.

9   Teaching aids, resources and ideas may be shared and plans made for their use.

)1   Individual student needs may be considered and general age group characteristics studied.

11   Pupil attendance records may be studied for information that could lead to ministering more effectively to each child and his home.

12   Approaches and plans for home ministry, including visitation, may be discussed and finalized.

13   More rapid orientation of new teaching personnel will result, and in-service training can be emphasized.

14   Personal needs of teachers and pupils may be shared in discussion and prayer.

15   Department superintendents may provide the leadership and guidance needed by their teachers, thus nurturing them in their service.

UNIT PLAN SHEETS

Both department superintendents and teachers will be assisted in their jobs by making detailed lesson plans for each unit of study including each particular lesson. Worksheets 1-4 at the end of this chapter provide useful guidelines for this purpose. It is recommended that the departmental officers meet together for planning at least one week prior to the beginning of each new unit of Bible study. The superintendent, following his own personal preparation, will lead the teachers in discussing the entire unit teaching thrust and will assist them in planning for their class and activity learning periods. The worksheets can be completed in this teachers meeting. Filling them in will help each leader to grasp the content, aims, methods and overall spiritual thrust of the study ahead of them. Moreover, it will allow them the opportunity to begin early to gather resources and activity materials necessary to the Bible study unit.

STUDY COURSES

Teacher training courses have played a primary role in the effective preparation of teachers. The usual approach of course studies has included a broad range of subjects, including the major areas of Bible and theology, age group characteristics and educational techniques.

If there is a weakness in this approach, it is probably that it fails to deal with educational techniques which tie into the particular teaching plan and curriculum used by the children's departments of the local church. For instance, a course study may make a teacher aware of the learning potential of creative writing, but the teacher's curriculum plan may not allow time for the use of this activity. On the other hand, the curriculum used may suggest that children be given the opportunity to choose a learning activity, but the training course may not provide the necessary information that would help the teaching personnel take this action.

Training courses and curriculum philosophy should work together harmoniously. This is the basis of producing teachers who understand and practice the teaching-learning plan that will produce the greatest results.

Your Sunday school will undoubtedly obtain many benefits as you digest thoroughly the contents of this book and its companion, *Ways to Help Them Learn: Children.* Both of these books present a unified philosophy of children's education but from different perspectives. *Ways to Plan and Organize Your Sunday School* deals with planning and organization, while *Ways to Help Them Learn* deals with age group characteristics and the corresponding learning philosophy and methods. We recommend that these books be studied by all children's workers, either in a class course study or on an individual basis.

Teachers selected to teach courses in childhood education should be competent in this field. Those who are not practitioners in Christian education of children will be ill-equipped to meet the practical needs and problems that your teachers will be confronted with, in the class sessions. The best person to teach such courses may be a children's department coordinator or skilled department superintendent.

A SUGGESTED MEETING PLAN

Not every church has definite plans regarding Sunday school teachers and officers meetings. Sometimes they are held only upon demand or preceding special calendar events, such as fall promotion and Christmas. Frequently individual departments meet on their own, rarely assembling with other teachers and officers in the school. A national survey showed that almost 28 percent of the churches surveyed held teachers meetings less than every third month, while over 23 percent met once or twice a month.[9]

It should be obvious that many churches do not meet and plan regularly enough to have successful teaching ministries. Advanced programs of children's education, like those recommended within this book, require more frequent planning sessions. Many churches have found that weekly meetings are a key to quality Christian education. They provide the opportunity for continuous teacher training, planning and preparation and assure effective teaching and learning on a week-to-week basis.

It is recommended that your department conduct at least a monthly planning meeting, preferably in conjunction with a meeting of all Sunday school teachers and officers in your church. The Sunday schools which hold frequent teachers' meetings are most often the stronger Sunday schools. This agency of church education is going to grow in size and quality, by providing the stimulation that comes from frequent teachers' meetings.

A monthly meeting may be difficult for some churches to initiate, but it is well worth the effort. Nothing of great spiritual worth has ever come about without the deliberate expending of human energies. "There is nothing easy about Sunday school," stated Dr. Mears. "It demands everything we have. It is a labor of prayer. It is a labor of intelligence. It is a labor of muscle."[10]

THREE TIME MODULES

Here is a practical plan which you may find applicable to your church's Sunday school program. A two-hour monthly workers' meeting or conference can be conducted on an evening suitable to the majority of personnel and the church calendar. The conference can be divided into three periods of time.

SUNDAY SCHOOL COUNCIL: The first period could run

from 7:00 to 7:30. During this time the Sunday school council meets. It is a group comprised of the following individuals: 1) the Sunday school superintendent; 2) the departmental superintendents; 3) the division coordinators; if there are any, and 4) the pastor and/or the director of Christian education.

There are certain business matters of interest to the Sunday school council:

1 Discussion of the overall calendar. At these sessions, dates which will affect the entire school, such as promotion or graduation plans, the annual picnic, attendance enlargement campaigns, Christmas program and the workers' appreciation banquet.

2 Discussion problem areas. Where are additional personnel needed? How will they be discovered, recruited and trained? Are there rooms which need to be remodeled or groups which need to switch rooms due to their size and growth patterns?

3 Communication and formulation of plans for the second period, the general session. What will compose the agenda of this second period? What calendar events need to be promoted? What information needs to be shared, discussed and applied in the individual department periods which follow?

GENERAL SESSION: The second time period, the general session, may run from 7:30 to 8:00. All Sunday school personnel—coordinators, superintendents, teachers, secretaries—should be present at this meeting. The following kinds of activities will generally compose this half-hour period: 1) the communication of information concerning the overall calendar of events which affect the entire school; 2) an inspirational talk or testimony from some leader, possibly your pastor; and 3) general motivation for more effective teaching, visitation and outreach.

DEPARTMENTAL SESSIONS: The third time period, the departmental session, will last about an hour—from 8:00 to 9:00. During this last period there are three primary activities:

1 The specific interpretation and application of the information communicated in the general session. For instance, if an attendance enlargement campaign has

been announced, in what way will the teachers in your department participate? Or if an all-Sunday-school visitation night has been promoted in the general session, the mechanics of the teachers' participation should be discussed.

2   the discussion and implementation of details concerning the care and growth of department attendance. Is the importance of regular pupil attendance being promoted? Are definite efforts being made to discover and reach prospective pupils? Is your follow-up of absentees efficient? Are efforts being made to reach the unchurched parents of your pupils? Are members and visitors made aware of upcoming social activities?

3   The preparation of units of study. The majority of the department period will usually be spent on this most important part of the monthly meeting. Teaching the Bible is the big business of Sunday school and requires in-depth planning. The worksheets clearly show the types of planning needed prior to the beginning of each unit.

OTHER TRAINING METHODS

Training of teachers should not be limited to one or two methods. Each church has the freedom and ability to come up with training ideas and plans suitable to its own situation. Don't limit your training potential and plan.

Many larger churches conduct their own annual leadership training institutes. Age group specialists are brought in to give help and instruction to every age division: early childhood, children, youth and adult. Smaller churches may find such a plan difficult unless it can be accomplished through the cooperative efforts of several churches in a given vicinity.

Observing competent teachers is an excellent training procedure. Many gifted children's teachers admit that they have learned best from observing other competent teachers. Nothing is more influential toward changing a teacher's pattern of instruction than seeing how a good teacher operates in a normal Sunday school session.

Visiting a department of another Sunday school which has demonstrated success effectively in teaching the Word of God should be encouraged as a requirement in learning how to teach well. Frequently such observation is accompanied by personal instruction and explanation by a trainer of teachers.

In-service training is another very effective means of preparing children's workers. The department superintendent providing this training should spend adequate time in counsel with each teacher-in-training. New teachers will have many questions, doubts and problems in their initial contact with the teaching procedures in the children's departments. The educational philosophy with which they are involved should be thoroughly explained. A weekly phone call by the department superintendent, in addition to the monthly workers meeting, and counsel before and after Sunday school sessions will help to nurture these teachers.

A summer reading of training manuals may be initiated in the children's division. This may culminate in a "write-up" session, held either at the church, a worker's home or at some retreat. At this time the participants would sit down and write the answers to the questions at the end of each chapter and share in the related discussion.

Area Sunday school conventions and workshops may also be useful in further equipping your teaching ministry.

One of the great needs of the work of Christ on earth through all of history has been, and is, the need for trained leadership. The task of providing such teachers and leaders for Christian education is a gigantic one. It is also a tremendously difficult task due to the complex and exacting nature of the discipline of Christian education.[11] To effectively teach our children to observe all of Christ's commandments, we must first train and equip our children's teachers in the best ways possible. More skill, time and energy must be given to this work if the Sunday school is going to make the spiritual impact that God intends for it in this decade.

Worksheet #1 (Department staff uses this sheet to plan together at staff meeting.)

TOTAL SESSION UNIT PLAN SHEET

(Bible Study, Bible Sharing/Planning, Bible Learning Activities*)

Title of Unit: _____ Dates:_____
Bible passages: _____
Persons and/or events in Bible passage: _____
Unit aim: That the students may (know, feel):

That the students may respond by:

Bible verses to know: _____
Songs to teach: _____

BIBLE STUDY* (Each teacher fills out worksheet #2 after department staff meeting)

BIBLE SHARING/PLANNING*

Date	Program for the day	Materials for superintendent

BIBLE LEARNING ACTIVITIES*

Activity	Teacher
1. _____	_____
2. _____	_____
3. _____	_____
4. _____	_____
5. _____	_____

*Based on the three blocks of time in teacher's/leader's manual.

Worksheet #2 (Each teacher uses this sheet to plan his specific responsibilities *after department staff meeting.*)

TEACHER UNIT WORKSHEET FOR *BIBLE STUDY*

Specific prayer requests/student needs to be met:

BUILDING READINESS ACTIVITIES			BIBLE STUDY		
Date Lesson	Activity	Materials	Scripture	Lesson Aims	Questions to relate Bible lesson to life
			Bible passage Bible characters and/or events Bible verse to know		
			Bible passage Bible characters and/or events Bible verse to know		
			Bible passage Bible characters and/or events Bible verse to know		
			Bible passage Bible characters and/or events Bible verse to know		
			Bible passage Bible characters and/or events Bible verse to know		

Worksheet #3   (Each teacher uses *one sheet per Bible Learning Activity* for which he will be responsible. Fill this sheet out *after* department staff meeting.)

TEACHER WORKSHEET FOR
BIBLE LEARNING ACTIVITIES

Bible Learning Activity: _____

Date(s): _____   For unit sharing? _____

Purpose: _____

_____

Materials: _____

_____

Procedures: _____

_____

Children who choose this activity: Responsibility:

1. _____   _____

2. _____   _____

3. _____   _____

4. _____   _____

5. _____   _____

6. _____   _____

7. _____   _____

8. _____   _____

Worksheet #4 (Each teacher hands in to department superintendent or person who handles orders. For optional use.)

ORDER BLANK

Requested by _____ Department_____

Item	Size	Color	Quantity	Date Needed
_____	____	____	____	____
_____	____	____	____	____
_____	____	____	____	____
_____	____	____	____	____
_____	____	____	____	____
_____	____	____	____	____
_____	____	____	____	____
_____	____	____	____	____
_____	____	____	____	____
_____	____	____	____	____
_____	____	____	____	____
_____	____	____	____	____
_____	____	____	____	____
_____	____	____	____	____
_____	____	____	____	____
_____	____	____	____	____
_____	____	____	____	____
_____	____	____	____	____
_____	____	____	____	____
_____	____	____	____	____
_____	____	____	____	____

FOOTNOTES

CHAPTER 7

1 · Eleanor L. Doan, compiler, *431 Quotes from the Notes of Henrietta C. Mears* (Glendale, Calif: Regal Books, 1970), p. 43.

2 · 1 Timothy 4:16, *King James Version.*

3 · 2 Timothy 2:15, *KJV.*

4 · "Yesterday, Today, and Forever," An interview with Wilbur M. Smith, *Decision* magazine, May 1971, p. 12.

5 · Barbara J. Bolton, *Ways to Help Them Learn, Children: Grades 1-6* (Glendale, Calif.: Regal Books, 1971).

6 · Scripture Press Ministries, Christian Education Division, *Research Report on Sunday School Teachers* (Wheaton, Ill.: Scripture Press, 1971), p. 26.

7 · Scripture Press Ministries, *Research Report on Sunday School Teachers,* p. 27.

8 · Scripture Press Ministries, *Research Report on Sunday School Teachers,* p. 28.

9 · Scripture Press Ministries, *Research Report on Sunday School Teachers,* p. 28.

10 · Doan, *431 Quotes from the Notes of Henrietta C. Mears,* p. 40.

11 · C. B. Eavey, *History of Christian Education* (Chicago: Moody Press, 1964), p. 421.

BIBLIOGRAPHY

American Sunday School Union. *The Teacher Taught.*
Philadelphia: American Sunday School Union, 1861.

Ashby, La Verne. "Primaries and Church Membership."
Baptist Training Union Magazine, March 1970, pp. 56-59.

Baker, Delores and Rives, Elsie. *Teaching the Bible
to Primaries.* Nashville: Convention Press, 1964.

Barnes, Albert. *Barnes' Notes on the New Testament.*
Grand Rapids: Kregel Publications, 1962.

Barth, Roland S. "When Children Enjoy School."
Childhood Education, Vol. 46, no. 4, January 1970, pp.
195-200.

Bayly, Joseph. *Christian Education Trends.*
Elgin, Ill.: David C. Cook Publishing Co., June 2, 1969.

Bolton, Barbara. *Ways to Help Them Learn, Children:
Grades 1-6.* Glendale, Calif.: Regal Books, 1971.

Broman, Betty L. "Too Much Shushing—Let Children Talk.
Childhood Education, vol. 46, no. 3, December 1969,
pp. 132-134.

Bowman, Locke E. *Straight Talk About Teaching in
Today's Church.* Philadelphia: Westminster Press, 1968.

Butler, J. Donald. *Religious Education, The Foundation
and Practice of Nurture.* New York: Harper and
Row Publishers, 1962.

Chamberlain, Eugene and Fullbright, Robert G. *Children's
Sunday School Work.* Nashville: Convention Press, 1969.

Clendinning, B. A., Jr., ed. *Family Ministry in Today's
Church.* Nashville: Convention Press, 1971.

Clouse, Bonnidell. "Psychosocial Origins of Stability
in the Christian Faith." *Christianity Today,*
September 25, 1970, pp. 12-14.

Cober, Kenneth L. *The Church's Teaching Ministry.*
Valley Forge, Pa.: Judson Press, 1964.

Cooperative Curriculum Project. *A Design for
Teaching-Learning.* St. Louis: Bethany Press, 1967.

Cully, Kendig Brubaker, ed. *Basic Writings
in Christian Education.* Philadelphia:
Westminster Press, 1960.

DeJong, Norman. *Education in the Truth.* Nuttey, N.J.:
Presbyterian and Reformed Publishing Co., 1969.

Doan, Eleanor L., ed. 431 *Quotes from the Notes of Henrietta C. Mears.* Glendale, Calif.:
Regal Books, 1970.

Eavey, C. B. *History of Christian Education.*
Chicago: Moody Press, 1964.

Fraser, David W. "What's Ahead for Preadolescence?",
Childhood Education, vol. 46, no. 1,
September-October, 1969, pp.24-28.

Frymier, Jack R. *Learning Centers: Children on Their Own.*
Washington, D.C.: The Association for Childhood
Education International, 1970.

Gregory, John Milton. *The Seven Laws of Teaching,*
Revised Edition. Grand Rapids: Baker Book House, 1962.

Harty, Robert A. *Children in Church Training.*
Nashville: Convention Press, 1969.

Horne, Herman Harrell. *Jesus—The Master Teacher.*
Grand Rapids: Kregel Publications, 1964.

Ingle, Clifford. *Children and Conversion.*
Nashville: Broadman Press, 1970

Jaarsma, Cornelius. *Human Development,
Learning and Teaching.* Grand Rapids: Wm. B. Eerdmans
Publishing Co., 1959

Jackson, B. F., Jr., ed. *Communication-Learning
for Churchmen, Volume 1.* Nashville:
Abingdon Press, 1968

James, Howard. *Children in Trouble: A National Scandal.*
New York: David McKay Co., 1970.

Jaroff, Leon, ed., Michaelis, Ingrid and others.
"The American Family: Future Uncertain." *Time,*
December 28, 1970, pp. 34-39.

Larson, Bruce. *No Longer Strangers.*
Waco: Word Books, 1971.

LeBar, Lois E. *Education That Is Christian.*
Westwood, N.J.: Fleming H. Revell Co., 1958.

Lederach, Paul M. *Reshaping the Teaching Ministry.*
Scottdale, Pa.: Herald Press, 1968.

LeShan, Eda J. *The Conspiracy Against Childhood.*
New York: Atheneum, 1967.

McNeil, Elton B. "The Changing Children of
Preadolescence."
Childhood Education, January 1970, pp. 181-185.

MollenKott, Virginia Ramey. "Teachers, Students
and Selfishness." *Christianity Today,*
April 24, 1970, pp. 13-15.

Osborn, D. Keith and Hale, William. "Television Violence."
Childhood Education, Vol. 45, no. 9, May 1969, pp. 505-507.

earce, Lucia. "Environmental Structure: A Third artner in Education." *Educational Technology,* eptember 15, 1968, p. 13.

rice, John M. *Jesus the Teacher.* Nashville: onvention Press, 1946.

ozell, Ray. *Talks on Sunday School Teaching.* rand Rapids: Zondervan Publishing House, 1956.

cripture Press Ministries, Christian Education ivision. *Research Report on Sunday School eachers.* Wheaton, Ill.: Scripture Press Publications, 1971.

olderholm, Marjorie. *Explaining Salvation to Children.* inneapolis: Free Church Publications, 1962.

mith, Wilbur. "Yesterday, Today and Forever." *ecision* magazine, May 1971, pp. 1,12.

erbeek, William R. *Frontiersmen of Faith,* "Story f the Prophets." Teacher's Study Guide nd Manual, Cathedral Films, n.d.

lich, Robert. *A History of Religious Education.* ew York: University Press, 1968.

farner, Wayne M. "Making Moving More Meaningful." *ome Life,* August 1970, pp. 28-30.

/yckoff, C. Campbell. *Theory and Design of Christian ducation-Curriculum.* Philadelphia: /estminster Press, 1961.

uck, Roy. *The Holy Spirit in Your Teaching.* /heaton: Scripture Press Publications, 1963.

:uck, Roy B. and Getz, Gene A. *Christian Youth, n In-Depth Study.* Chicago: Moody Press, 1968.

he publishers do not necessarily endorse the entire contents of all the ublications referred to in this book.

Train for Effective Leadership

The impact of effective leadership can be felt in every area of your Sunday school. Train your leaders and teachers with **Success Handbooks** from ICL. Prepared by recognized authorities in Christian education, the handbooks in each series are especially designed for four basic age groups:
Early Childhood, Children, Youth, Adult.

Series 1, Ways to Help Them Learn
The Success Handbook on each level discusses the learning process, age characteristics, needs and abilities, plus proven teaching techniques.

Series 2, Ways to Plan and Organize Your Sunday School
The Success Handbook on each level offers guidance in building your Sunday school with a plan consistent and effective at every level.

Each Success Handbook $1.95.
Boxed set of all 8: $14.95.

Regal Books
Glendale, California